TExES

Pedagogy and Professional Responsibilities EC-12 Practice Questions

Dear Future Exam Success Story:

First of all, **THANK YOU** for purchasing Mometrix study materials!

Second, congratulations! You are one of the few determined test-takers who are committed to doing whatever it takes to excel on your exam. **You have come to the right place.** We developed these practice tests with one goal in mind: to deliver you the best possible approximation of the questions you will see on test day.

Standardized testing is one of the biggest obstacles on your road to success, which only increases the importance of doing well in the high-pressure, high-stakes environment of test day. Your results on this test could have a significant impact on your future, and these practice tests will give you the repetitions you need to build your familiarity and confidence with the test content and format to help you achieve your full potential on test day.

Your success is our success

We would love to hear from you! If you would like to share the story of your exam success or if you have any questions or comments in regard to our products, please contact us at **800-673-8175** or **support@mometrix.com**.

Thanks again for your business and we wish you continued success!

Sincerely,
The Mometrix Test Preparation Team

TABLE OF CONTENTS

Practice Test #1

1. Which of the following is a common symptom of spina bifida?
    a. Motor dyspraxia/apraxia
    b. Lower-body paresis
    c. Athetosis
    d. Spasticity

2. The school district in which Mr. Copeland teaches seventh grade language arts is in a low-income community with a high adult illiteracy rate, and he knows that the parents of many of his students can only read on an elementary school level. While many of the parents are very engaged in their students' education, they're not able to help their children with reading assignments at home. What is the first step Mr. Copeland should take to ensure that all of his students receive support in completing their reading homework?
    a. He should identify parents who struggle with reading and help them enroll in a local adult literacy program so that they can learn to read and eventually help their students with homework
    b. He should attempt to create a tutoring program in which older students and literate parents volunteer to provide homework support after school or during lunch
    c. He should personally provide tutoring to parents who struggle with reading
    d. He should eliminate homework assignments altogether or provide easier assignments for the students who lack homework support

3. All but which of the following are critical values that are formed during the middle school years?
    a. Respect for diversity
    b. Commitment to continued schooling
    c. Tolerance of those who are different
    d. Higher-order thinking skills

4. If you decide to allow your students to check their own homework in class, which method of recording grades should not be used?
    a. Collect the graded assignments and record them yourself
    b. Have the students call out the grades to you from their desks
    c. Walk around the room and visually check the grades yourself
    d. Have a teacher's aide record the grades

5. Among strategies that the U.S. Department of Education (ED) includes in its model for parent involvement, which is described accurately?
    a. Communicating not about teacher qualifications, but rather about data for accountability
    b. Training parents to help children achieve academically rather than influence school policy
    c. Emphasizing parental involvement opportunities over supplemental educational services
    d. Communicating with parents only in English, always using uniform, standardized formats

6. Informed by research results, experts on conflict resolution recommend which of the following as good listening behaviors for teachers to impart to students?
    a. Asking questions as needed, but not interrupting others
    b. Avoiding embarrassing others by not making eye contact
    c. Giving others suggestions or advice about what they said
    d. Staying objective by not nodding/smiling as others speak

1

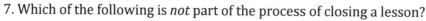

7. Which of the following is *not* part of the process of closing a lesson?
   a. Extended practice.
   b. Review of key points.
   c. Preview of future lessons.
   d. Demonstration of student work.

8. Strategies for establishing a logical-mathematical learning environment include all except which one of the following?
   a. Conducting interviews
   b. Venn diagrams
   c. Thinking of probabilities
   d. Discerning patterns

9. Mrs. Frances wants to develop a theme-based unit that is interesting and relevant to her fifth grade students. Which of the following approaches would be most likely to help her achieve this goal?
   a. Send a note to the students' parents asking them what theme their children should learn about
   b. Review the success of theme-based units that were used by the students' teachers in previous years
   c. Conduct an informal, open-ended survey to look for interests that the students share
   d. Present three different theme ideas as ask the students to vote on the one that will be used in class

10. If the students in your class have radically varied levels of skill and knowledge, which technique will make your class more manageable?
   a. Choose a medium level of instruction that you believe will work for most of the class
   b. Break the class up into several small groups, divided by skill level, and give appropriate assignments to each group
   c. Teach your class to the highest skill level, and then offer help after class to those who cannot keep up
   d. Ask the smartest students to transfer to a more advanced class, and the weakest students to transfer to a remedial class

11. How can including cooperative learning strategies in the classroom teach practical life skills to students?
   a. Students learn to work independently, even when others are around.
   b. Students learn interpersonal problem-solving skills that they will need later in life.
   c. Students learn ways to score better on standardized tests.
   d. Students learn the importance of physical exercise in their daily lives.

12. Effective teacher strategies for organizing and managing learning environments that result in high student engagement and low misbehavior include which of these?
   a. Alerting student attention through a focus on the entire class
   b. Concealing teacher awareness of student behavior from them
   c. Designing and implementing activities without any overlapping
   d. Having instruction proceed steadily without adding momentum

2

13. What is a disadvantage of using rubrics as assessment tools?
    a. Learning objectives, tasks, guidance, and criteria are combined.
    b. Performance levels are not as precise as grades or percentages.
    c. They afford greater brevity in definition, guidance, assessment.
    d. Rubrics are more concise yet offer more clarity than other tools.

14. Which of the following is a good example of a learning goal that a teacher should set for a poetry unit in an English literature class?
    a. Students will learn to identify the most common meters used in English literature, with a focus being placed upon iambic pentameter
    b. Students will learn to appreciate and enjoy poetry as an art form
    c. Students will learn how to identify the elements of good poetry
    d. Students will learn the cultural importance of poetry to English speakers around the world

15. According to research findings, which of these predict(s) parents' involvement in their children's education the most?
    a. Racial or ethnic status of parents
    b. The marital status of the parents
    c. The educational levels of parents
    d. School policies, teacher practices

16. At the end of the year, the teachers decide that they want to evaluate the effectiveness of the team-teaching model for their sixth grade students. Which of the following research strategies would provide them with the best assessment of the model?
    a. The teachers should compare this group of students' performance on standardized tests in previous years with their performance in sixth grade at the end of the year
    b. The teachers should compare the students' performance in classes that are part of the team teaching model (math, science, language arts, social studies) with their performance in classes that are not team-taught (health, physical education, art)
    c. The teachers should compare their students' performance in sixth grade to the performance of sixth grade students at schools that do not use team teaching
    d. The teachers should compare their sixth grade students' performance this year with the performance of sixth grade students in previous years where team teaching was not used; they should also consider the performance history of this particular group of sixth graders relative to previous groups.

17. Mr. Mailer recommends that Thomas, a student in his fourth grade class, be assessed for a possible reading disability, but Thomas' parents are strongly resistant to this idea. They say that Thomas is just a "late bloomer," and that testing him for a reading disability will only erode his self-esteem. They insist that the test be put off at least until next year to see if Thomas improves. How should Mr. Mailer respond to Thomas' parents' resistance to his conviction that Thomas needs to be considered for special education services?

    a. Since parents understand their children's needs best, he should simply agree to wait until next year

    b. He should have Thomas tested anyway, and let the parents know the results only if Thomas qualifies for special education services

    c. He should refer the matter to the school principal to avoid possible legal repercussions

    d. He should explain to the parents that the decision is ultimately theirs, but he should also provide them with educational resources about reading disabilities and emphasize that delaying receipt of special education services can exacerbate the problems associated with reading disabilities

18. How can a teacher ensure that all students are contributing equally during cooperative learning exercises?

    a. The teacher should circulate among the groups and observe how they are working together.

    b. Assign one student in each group to monitor student participation

    c. Assign each student in each group a specific task to accomplish

    d. Avoid such exercises, since they inevitably end up with one or two students doing most of the work

19. Ms. Mattingly has received her fourth grade class' standardized test results, and they show that her students are significantly behind the other fourth grade classes in the district in both reading and math. She didn't realize her students were so far behind, because they had been doing well on in-class assessments. How should Ms. Mattingly respond to this situation?

    a. Since standardized tests are an imperfect measure of achievement, she should ignore the results as long as her students are doing well in her class

    b. She should confer with her principal and other fourth grade teachers to determine whether her grade level expectations for academic achievement align with those of the district as a whole

    c. She should change her instructional methods to "teach to the test" and include more practice taking multiple choice tests for her students

    d. She should send a letter to her students' parents informing them that their children need tutoring in reading and math

20. In what areas do computers have the least benefit for student learning?

    a. Simple drills presented, such as teaching multiplication tables. This frees up the teacher to work with the students on developing higher-level skills.

    b. Role-playing games that develop greater social awareness and that allow the students to participate more directly in the events they are learning about

    c. Simulations of mechanical activities that help the students develop motor skills and reflexes

    d. Exercises that teach higher-order thinking and professional skills

21. Which form of teacher body language is most likely to promote misbehavior in class?

    a. Teacher looks students directly in the eye when speaking
    b. Teacher speaks in a calm assertive tone
    c. Teacher stands with back straight and head held high
    d. Teacher keeps eyes focused on her book and speaks very softly

22. Which of the following is a valid technique to use with non-native English speakers in your class if they are having trouble and your school has very limited ESL resources?

    a. Ask the student's parents to hire a translator to sit with the child in class
    b. Use more visual aids and illustrative hand gestures while teaching
    c. Speak as rapidly as possible so that the student will get used to hearing English faster
    d. Repeat everything you say twice

23. Which of these is NOT one of the major personality structures proposed by Sigmund Freud in his psychoanalytic theory of development?

    a. Id
    b. Ego
    c. Libido
    d. Superego

24. When teaching Shakespeare's *Romeo and Juliet*, which technique might help students maintain interest despite the difficult language?

    a. Give the students a glossary of archaic English words commonly found in the play
    b. Include a discussion of some modern interpretations of the story (movies such as *Romeo+Juliet*, or even *West Side Story*) and have students identify differences between the modern versions and the original
    c. Have the students read the parts out loud
    d. Hold a detailed discussion of English syntax and grammar of the period

25. Mr. Robinson, a fifth grade teacher, wants to improve his students' motivation by showing them that math and reading skills can be used to learn about important subjects like the environment, history, or multiculturalism. The best approach to achieve this objective would be to:

    a. Ask students to conduct an independent research project on a topic of their choice
    b. Have students practice math and reading skills in groups
    c. Present a thematic unit that incorporates math and reading skills
    d. Use curriculum-based methods to assess students' progress in math and reading

26. Mrs. Alito has a student in her class who has been diagnosed with anxiety disorder. Sometimes the student becomes so anxious in class that he needs to go to the special education resource room for brief periods. How can Mrs. Alito best meet the student's needs without making him feel uncomfortable or disrupting the rest of her class?

    a. She can quietly check in with the student once every few hours to see if he is feeling especially anxious
    b. She can ask him to raise his hand and ask to be excused if he is feeling anxious
    c. She can teach him relaxation exercises so that he does not need to leave the class
    d. She can keep an eye on the student and provide him with a nonverbal signal that he can use to alert her if he needs to go to the resource room

5

27. What is the most accurate indicator of overall student performance?
    a. Final exams and other tests that cover course material on a comprehensive basis.
    b. The combined results of frequent evaluations given throughout the term.
    c. Studies show that in the end, a teacher's gut instinct about at student is usually right.
    d. Homework and papers are usually the best indicator, since they show how a student thinks when not under direct teacher supervision.

28. Mr. Ivanov has several students in his class whose parents have recently immigrated to the United States and who are not comfortable conversing in English. The parents' native language is Spanish, and Mr. Ivanov does not speak Spanish. In order to ensure that these parents can participate in the upcoming parent-teacher conferences, which of the following steps should Mr. Ivanov take first?
    a. He should ask the Spanish-speaking students if they would be willing to serve as translators for the conferences
    b. He should send a note to the parents informing them that they will need to hire a translator if they want to participate in the conferences
    c. He should inform the school principal that he cannot hold the conferences if he is not supplied with a translator
    d. He should find someone to help him write a note to the parents in Spanish explaining that he will help them find a volunteer translator if they do not have a friend or family member who could translate for them

29. Based on teacher experience, what is a strategy for effective parent-teacher conferences?
    a. Beginning each conference with improvements needed
    b. Sandwiching every criticism between two positive items
    c. Relieving parents of preparatory papers to read or write
    d. Excluding student works that will only distract parents

30. When dealing with a class with widely varied levels of skill and knowledge, what common pitfall is most harmful?
    a. Giving too much attention to the weaker students
    b. Permitting the stronger students to correct the weaker students in class
    c. Offering more encouragement to the stronger students than the weaker students
    d. Overcorrecting the mistakes of the weaker students

31. Ellen, a student, has been diagnosed with a serious illness and will be out of school for several months. Ellen's parents have asked her teachers to send her worksheets home to her in electronic form. All but which of the following could be used to send electronic copies of paper worksheets?
    a. Copy machine
    b. Scanner
    c. Flash drive or disc
    d. Email

32. Which teacher characteristic will best help facilitate student cooperation in the classroom?
    a. Rigid military-style discipline
    b. Consistency in how rules are enforced
    c. A playful, loving approach, even when rules are broken
    d. Ignore misbehavior so that the students will see that they can't get to you

33. Mrs. Sanchez is a new teacher of 9th grade literature. She truly loves her subject, and the highlight of each class period is when she holds a 20-minute class discussion of the previous day's reading assignment. She is very enthusiastic about these discussions and encourages the students to form and express their own opinions. She often asks provocative questions and pushes the students to consider the motives of characters from different points of view. Many of the students enjoy this, but an observer notices some problems. Misbehavior by a few students is getting out of hand. And a couple of students seem to just zone out. What common mistake is Mrs. Sanchez making?

a. She is not being strict enough.
b. She is devoting too much time to discussions.
c. She is concentrating all her attention on the discussions and not noticing everything that is going on in the classroom.
d. Her enthusiasm makes her look weak to the students.

34. How should a teacher initially plan to manage a highly diverse classroom?

a. On the first day of class, the teacher should ask each student to complete a survey to determine the students' cultural, ethnic, and racial background.
b. A good teacher should be intimately familiar with the major cultures within the local school district.
c. A teacher should plan lessons so that new material is introduced using a variety of different approaches.
d. Guest teachers from different ethnic backgrounds should occasionally be invited to teach, so that all students will feel more comfortable.

35. What has been determined through research about family involvement in education?

a. Family involvement improves student self-esteem without affecting students' attitudes.
b. Family involvement has been found through research to benefit each of these variables.
c. Family involvement is found to improve students' attendance rather than their behavior.
d. Family involvement raises student test scores and grades but not post-secondary school.

36. A tenured teacher who coaches and advocates academically, serves as an example of lifelong learning, and often may stay at this level throughout the teaching career is identified by which U.S. Department of Education (ED) term?

a. Professional Teacher
b. Resident Teacher
c. Master Teacher
d. Teacher Leader

37. Piaget described children as "little scientists" interacting and experimenting with the environment to learn about it and actively build their own knowledge. This reflects which type of philosophy and psychology?

a. Scaffolding
b. Cognitivism
c. Constructivism
d. Zone of Proximal Development

38. Among the following auditory disabilities, which one does not involve any part of the hearing mechanism?
    a. Only sensorineural-type hearing loss
    b. The conductive form of hearing loss
    c. Central auditory processing disorder
    d. The condition of complete deafness

39. What is most true about how field trips relate to student learning?
    a. Their only benefit is that students love getting out of the classroom.
    b. They have the benefits of applying classroom knowledge in real life.
    c. They confuse students when real conditions differ from classrooms.
    d. They give the benefit of interacting with nature but offer no real learning.

40. When assigning large student projects, such as term papers of research projects, what is the most effective system for evaluation?
    a. When the project is over, assign a single overall grade. This will teach the students what to expect in college.
    b. Grade the projects on a curve
    c. The projects should be evaluated as work progresses and according to multiple standards, including overall accuracy, timely completion of individual steps, quality of research, grammar and spelling, etc.
    d. Projects should be graded on a simple pass/fail basis, since the overall experience is more important than the quality of the result.

41. Which of the following is a characteristic of indirect instruction?
    a. It is delivered explicitly.
    b. It has uniform lesson plans.
    c. It is more structured by nature.
    d. It involves exploratory activities.

42. Which of the following categories of cognitive disabilities most consistently includes the characteristic of a marked gap between intellectual ability and school performance?
    a. Autism spectrum disorders (ASDs)
    b. Intellectual disabilities (ID)
    c. None of these includes such a gap
    d. Specific learning disabilities (SLDs)

43. Which of the following teacher behaviors impedes rather than promotes school-home communication?
    a. Listening to the parents and/or families of students
    b. Mutually exchanging teacher and family expertise
    c. Instructing parents and/or families in what to do
    d. Brainstorming supportive strategies together

44. Which of the following statements most accurately describes the academic potential of students in low-income schools?

    a. They will fall irreversibly behind their wealthier peers because of lack of parental support and resources

    b. They should be presented with lower expectations since they will not need high-level academic skills for their future careers

    c. They may have a poor perception of their academic ability, but this disadvantage can be overcome with effective instruction and high expectations

    d. They cannot succeed academically unless their schools and communities are given vastly greater economic resources

45. Which teacher behaviors reflect strategies for supporting education through partnering with the families of students?

    a. Inviting parents by building rapport at the beginning of the year

    b. Being considerate of parents by only contacting about problems

    c. Respecting parents by not giving advice about the home settings

    d. Respecting family privacy by not prying into their lives and needs

46. Should students be allowed to use word processors to prepare written class assignments?

    a. No. Word processors discourage students from learning grammar and spelling. It is better for teachers to require students to hand write or type their assignments.

    b. The use of word processors should be mandatory on all written assignments and at all levels.

    c. No. Word processors are commercial products, and it is inappropriate for a teacher to encourage or require students to use one piece of software instead of another.

    d. Generally yes, but this depends on the nature of the assignment and the grade level of the class.

47. It is your first week of class teaching a 12th grade history class. Because of the subject matter, and because most of these students will be going on to college, a significant portion of the course will be presented in the form of college-style lectures. How can you ensure that all of the students have the necessary note-taking skills they will need, both for this class and beyond?

    a. This is not your responsibility. Since they are college-bound seniors, they should already have these skills.

    b. Give a pop quiz at the end of every class

    c. Give a lecture on note-taking on the first day of class

    d. Inform the students that for the first couple of weeks, you will collect their notes at the end of class and give them back the next day with corrections

48. Which behavior indicates a child has attained understanding of symbolic representation?

    a. Seeking unseen things

    b. Playing "make-believe"

    c. Enjoying "peek-a-boo"

    d. Addition using pennies

49. What is true about how teachers can support student development of intrinsic motivation?

    a. Teachers can interest students in content without being interested in it themselves.

    b. Teachers strongly interested in content need not show it to develop this motivation.

    c. Teachers can develop intrinsic student motivation without knowing student interests.

    d. Teachers can develop intrinsic motivation by connecting content to student interests.

50. How do teachers inform classroom behavior management with understanding of group dynamics, specifically individual students' group roles?

a. They develop friendly relationships with student leaders, instigators, and consciences.
b. They develop friendly relationships with student enforcers, procurers, and negotiators.
c. They develop strategies for keeping student leaders, procurers, and negotiators on-task.
d. They develop friendly relationships and on-task strategies for students in all these roles.

51. As a cognitive element of the learning process, what is a characteristic of planning?

a. Planning requires concrete thinking, not abstract thinking.
b. Planning requires both abstract thinking and imagination.
c. Planning requires organizational, not imaginative abilities.
d. Planning is on a lower level of higher-order thinking skills.

52. Research-based strategies to motivate students are reflected by which teacher behavior?

a. They are interested in students' learning but are not personally interested.
b. They are role models, leading student motivation and passion by example.
c. They need not believe in students' abilities as long as they indicate interest.
d. They eschew the personalization of subject content for individual students.

53. In the process of determining the rationale of an objective, the teacher should ask all of the following except:

a. Does this objective have an important learning outcome?
b. Will this objective fit my planned activity?
c. Will my students be able to use this knowledge in the future?
d. Are the prior knowledge and skill levels of my students sufficient to achieve this objective?

54. A new student, Jethro, has been assigned to your class. Jethro comes from a much rougher neighborhood than most of the students in your class and is having a very hard time fitting in. He often seems angry, and he speaks insolently both to you and to his classmates. It always seems that he has something to prove, and anytime he knows an answer in class, he hurriedly blurts it out, as though he is competing with the other students. His behavior is steadily becoming worse, and some of the other students seem to be afraid of him. When you correct his behavior in class he seems to be proud of himself, and becomes even more insolent. Which of the following would be a good first step to get through to him?

a. Put him in a seat by himself in the corner of the room
b. Point out to him in front of the class that his behavior is interfering with the entire class
c. Send him to the vice principal's office each time he misbehaves
d. Do not let him get away with anything, but make a point to always discipline him in private

55. As an approach for managing student behavior, what is a characteristic of the "simple authority statement" from the teacher?

a. It causes emotional distress but stops misbehavior authoritatively.
b. It models reasonable, respectful use of authority with little upset.
c. It expresses teacher disapproval of student behavior subjectively.
d. It expresses teacher disapproval authoritatively, but it takes time.

56. Of the following, which is an advantage of using analytical checklists for assessment?

    a. They allow for differences in assessing individual tasks across students.
    b. They require additional notes to identify other notable feats observed.
    c. They save time and effort by listing tasks, skills, or behaviors in advance.
    d. They sometimes constrain assessment to Yes/No without quality levels.

57. What kinds of teacher questions will get students actively involved in lesson content?

    a. Only cognitively lower-level questions requiring students to remember and understand
    b. Only higher-level questions requiring students to apply, analyze, evaluate, and synthesize
    c. Cognitively lower-level and higher-level questions can elicit active student involvement
    d. Cognitively lower-level or higher-level questions will not get students actively involved

58. Which of these is true about how family dynamics interact with parental participation in student education?

    a. Custody arrangements can complicate availability and participation.
    b. The work schedules of most parents will not significantly interfere.
    c. Among considerations for parents, transportation is rarely an issue.
    d. The number of children in a family has little impact on participation.

59. In today's public schools, who are most often responsible for instructing special education students?

    a. Educational specialists
    b. Special education teachers
    c. The most applicable therapists
    d. The regular classroom teachers

60. Ms. Carleton receives a phone call from one of her sixth grade students' parents. The parent is concerned that her daughter is performing poorly in language arts class, even though she has done well in this subject in the past. Ms. Carleton knows that this student has regularly failed to turn in homework assignments. How should Ms. Carleton respond to this parent's concerns?

    a. She should tell the parent that her daughter clearly doesn't understand the course content, and needs a tutor
    b. She should explain to the parent that her daughter isn't turning in homework assignments, and tell her to make sure that her daughter does so in the future
    c. She should tell the parent that, unfortunately, the Federal Educational Right to Privacy Act (FERPA) prevents her from discussing her students' academic records without their permission
    d. She should explain to the parent that her daughter has missed several homework assignments, and offer to tell the parent about future assignments so that she can ensure that her daughter completes them

61. Ms. Andrews has recently learned that she will have a student in her class whose family is currently living in a local homeless shelter. The teacher's most important responsibility to this student is to:

    a. Ensure that she creates an accepting, non-judgmental classroom environment
    b. Screen the new student to see if special education services are needed
    c. Determine whether the student suffers from depression or anxiety disorder
    d. Make sure that the student has adequate food and clothing

62. A fifth grade teacher has a mainstreamed special education student in her class who has a behavioral disability. The student has become increasingly disruptive over the past few weeks. Which of the following steps should the teacher take first in attempting to resolve this situation?

a. The teacher should call the student's parents and ask them to speak with the student about her behavior
b. The teacher should send the student to the principal's office when the disruptive behavior occurs
c. The teacher should discuss the problem with the special education teacher
d. The teacher should isolate the student so that her class is not disrupted

63. Which of the following describes a student who is a verbal-linguistic learner?

a. Likes field trips and physical exercise
b. Exhibits balance and dexterity
c. Shows a knack for learning other languages.
d. Adept at logical problem-solving

64. Suppose you are teaching a 10th grade U.S. government unit on the role and structure of Congress, and many of your students are slow to understand the workings of the U.S. Senate vs. the House of Representatives. Which of the following methods would be the most likely way to ensure that your students become more interested in the subject matter and take away from your class a practical understanding of the material?

a. Have the students take turns reading the textbook aloud in class
b. Assign each student to make a presentation on the biography of a current U.S. senator or congress person
c. Ask the students to follow the news closely at home, and to identify ongoing activities in Congress that you can discuss in class
d. Supplement the textbook material with charts and graphs to help the students better visualize the percentages of votes needed to pass a bill or override a veto

65. Mr. Kelley is teaching social studies class about World War II, and he engages his class in a discussion about how U.S. involvement in the war affected ordinary Americans. What is the primary educational benefit of engaging in this discussion?

a. It will help students remember important details about the war, such as dates of important events and names of important historical figures
b. It will help develop students' higher-order thinking skills
c. It will help students use their own experiences to understand social studies concepts
d. It will help develop students' sense of patriotism

66. Among school personnel, who is most likely to help classroom teachers by informing them about activities for developing fine motor and daily living skills?

a. Physical therapist
b. Occupational therapist
c. Special education staff
d. Any IEP team member

67. Grades 2-12 ELL students at the Intermediate Reading and Writing levels can do which of the following?

    a. Comprehend connected complex sentences on new subjects
    b. Communicate ideas in writing about unfamiliar abstract topics
    c. Read text in connected sentences fluently without rereading
    d. Write so readers familiar with ELL writing partially understand

68. When teachers assess student performance using continua, which is a disadvantage?

    a. More precise evaluative descriptions of student performance instead of discrete grades
    b. Greater difficulty in comparing student, class, and school scores without exact numbers
    c. Performance ranges are more realistic and accurate than exact numbers or cutoff scores
    d. Greater compatibility with individualized student assessment than standardized testing

69. What is most accurate regarding the work of para-educators in school classrooms?

    a. They are only permitted to perform concrete services.
    b. They typically work in classrooms on a volunteer basis.
    c. They perform tasks for the therapists without training.
    d. They can work with individual students in a one-on-one format.

70. How can teachers establish positive, productive learning environments for students whose developmental levels vary within the same classroom?

    a. Observe levels/types of children's play and provide only activities matching these.
    b. Give older elementary and middle school students high school-type collaboration.
    c. Do not expect new preschoolers' sharing, but do model, encourage, and reward it.
    d. Confine productive learning environments in high school classes to the classrooms.

71. Of the following, which represents descriptor for English Language Learners at the Intermediate proficiency level in Speaking?

    a. Speaking in simple sentences without need for hesitation
    b. Speaking in detailed sentences with sufficient vocabulary
    c. Speaking in simple sentences with mostly present tenses
    d. Speaking in sentences people unused to ELLs understand

72. What is most true about the relationship of teaching and classroom management?

    a. Teacher management decisions are more complex when instruction is more demanding.
    b. Encouraging student responsibility changes student behavior without affecting content.
    c. When students solve novel problems and create products, teacher decisions are simpler.
    d. Teachers focus on helping students meet academic demands instead of social demands.

73. What most reflects factors that can interfere with diverse parent and family communication and participation in the education of their children?

    a. Language barriers rarely stop parents/families from communicating.
    b. Parents with unsuccessful school histories try harder to participate.
    c. Families can be alienated from school processes because of culture.
    d. Poor past school experiences induce parents to help their children.

74. Which of the following is true of students whose parents are highly aware of and involved in their academic progress?

    a. They are always from high-income families
    b. They typically perform better in school than students whose families are less involved
    c. They are always near the top of their classes
    d. They are typically lower-performing students, because parents are only interested in their children's academic progress if they are not doing well

75. Ms. Kincaid has sent home a note with her fourth grade students asking their parents to sign up for parent-teacher conferences, but after a week, only about ten percent of the students' parents have done so. Ms. Kincaid is concerned that if a student's parents fail to attend a conference this will negatively impact the student's academic achievement. What is the first step that she should take in order to increase the number of parents who attend conferences?

    a. Take the students whose parents have not scheduled conferences aside and ask them whether or not they gave their parents the note about parent-teacher conferences
    b. Call the parents directly and notify them about the upcoming conferences
    c. Give the students another note to take home that emphasizes the importance of conferences to the students' academic development
    d. Tell the students that their grades will suffer if they don't convince their parents to attend the conference

76. Mrs. Lindsey frequently engages her fifth grade science class in structured problem solving activities. The main benefit of such activities for older elementary and middle-level students is that they:

    a. Foster inquiry and critical thinking skills
    b. Improve organizational and time-management skills
    c. Enhance students' social skills
    d. Teach students to appreciate diversity

77. Which of the following descriptions of adolescent behavior is an example of how behaviorist learning theory explains human development?

    a. A student sees struggling students getting more teacher attention and stops studying hard.
    b. A student sees others getting higher grades and more praise and then begins studying hard.
    c. A student sees high grades and praise coming from the teacher and continues studying hard.
    d. A student sees struggling students get less attention and decides to continue studying hard.

78. Which of the following is an example of a teacher using differentiation in the classroom?

    a. Ms. Morse divides her students into ability groups and spends at least one hour each week working with this group in a way that meets the members' unique needs
    b. Mr. Stillwell only holds parent-teacher conferences with the parents of students who are struggling in his class
    c. Mr. Karl and presents each of his reading lessons in ways that target the various academic levels and learning styles of his students
    d. Mrs. Tanner asks her math class to complete an assignment in groups, each of which contains at least one student who has demonstrated mastery of the material

79. Which of the following is the strongest signal for getting students' attention before starting a lesson?
    a. Say "Good morning."
    b. Say "Let's get started."
    c. Ring a bell.
    d. Use a hand signal for silence.

80. A survey conducted by a local newspaper reports that most parents of middle school students think that bullying is very common among adolescent boys, but unlikely to occur among girls. What is the most likely explanation for this misconception?
    a. The survey respondents were disproportionately male
    b. The parents who were surveyed do not participate in school-related activities or monitor their children's social development closely
    c. Parents are less likely to recognize bullying among girls because it is usually conducted through gossip and exclusion, rather than outright violence
    d. The level of violence at the school is so high that parents didn't notice the bullying that occurs among girls

81. After a month of class, Mr. Gupta notices that his 12th grade physics class has fallen well behind his planned curriculum. In-class experiments and other activities have taken significantly longer to complete than the teacher expected. What should he do?
    a. Cease holding in-class experiments and stick rigidly with following the units in the textbook
    b. Ignore the planned curriculum; the students will learn more from doing the experiments than from lectures and written assignments.
    c. Increase the amount of homework in order to catch up
    d. Evaluate way students are carrying out experiments and develop more organized procedures to keep the students on track

82. You are covering the American Revolution and the formation of the United States in your 10th grade U.S. history class. Which task would NOT help your students process what they are learning?
    a. Have the students write an essay on how the ideas of the founding fathers continue to influence us today
    b. Have each of the students memorize a different part of the Constitution or the Declaration of Independence and recite it before the class
    c. Ask the students to keep a learning log in which each day they write a short paragraph about the meaning of what they learned in class that day
    d. Assign each student to research and prepare an oral presentation on one of the founding fathers or another important figure of the time

83. Among these, what is a disadvantage of using scoring guides in assessment?
    a. Scoring guides are published by different authors than the tests they accompany.
    b. Scoring guides force teachers to give specific scores to specific student responses.
    c. Scoring guides can be misinterpreted/misapplied by inexperienced/unwise users.
    d. Scoring guides give teachers flexibility to use judgment with responses/conditions.

84. Among characteristics of intrinsic student motivation, which is an advantage?
    a. The length of time that it lasts
    b. The length of time that it takes
    c. The differentiation that it needs
    d. The length of time that it works

85. When a student is able to consider whether an information source is reputable, has been proven objectively, and is accepted by experts in its discipline, which element of critical thinking does the student demonstrate?
    a. Evaluating supporting evidence
    b. Judging the quality of material
    c. Distinguishing fact from opinion
    d. Finding evidence/no evidence

86. Which of the following factors is/are NOT a component of intrinsic motivation to learn?
    a. Fascination for the content
    b. Rewards and punishments
    c. Relevance to one's real life
    d. Enhancement of cognition

87. Mrs. Eli is holding a career day for her fifth grade class of 25 students, and has invited parents to come to class and discuss their jobs. Many parents have expressed interest, but most of them have said that they will have difficulty leaving their jobs during the school day. All but which of the following technological solutions might be helpful in addressing this problem?
    a. Holding the presentation by videoconference during the parent's their lunch break
    b. Holding the presentation by teleconference during the parent's lunch break
    c. Asking the parent to create a videotape in which they discuss their job and sending it to school
    d. Asking the parent to create a Powerpoint presentation about their job for their child to present to the class

88. Research studies have identified which teacher behaviors are based on different expectations of students?
    a. Teachers ask equally challenging questions of low-expectancy students.
    b. Teachers call on low-expectancy and high-expectancy students equally.
    c. Teachers go into less depth exploring low-expectancy student answers.
    d. Teachers reward less rigorous answers from low-expectancy students.

89. The emotional balance of a classroom can be upset by conflict. Appropriate methods for a teacher to use in handling conflict do not include:
    a. Gathering information and re-capping the situation.
    b. Allowing children to come up with a solution themselves.
    c. Letting the issue drop once a solution has been agreed upon.
    d. Dealing with the conflict calmly and with a quiet voice.

90. When students have been involved in classroom conflicts, what does it accomplish for teachers to have them write about these?
    a. It makes them ruminate about and extend conflicts.
    b. It gives them time out for cooling off and reflecting.
    c. It helps them review their feelings, not alternatives.
    d. It keeps them from learning anything from conflicts.

91. How are teachers required to ensure educational equity?
    a. By delivering uniform instruction to all students
    b. By offering different opportunities to students
    c. By treating students less fairly if they deserve it
    d. By using materials reflecting multicultural views

92. Ms. Frank conducts an assessment and discovers that most students in her fourth grade class are auditory learners, while a few are visual or kinesthetic learners. When teaching students a new concept, which of the following strategies would be most effective for the largest number of her students?
    a. Having her students write an explanation of the new concept in their own words
    b. Teaching the students a song that explains the new concept
    c. Writing an explanation of the new concept on the chalkboard
    d. Teaching the students to describe the concept using sign language

93. What is the correct meaning of cognitive dissonance?
    a. A cognitive processing disorder affecting understanding
    b. A disruption of cognition caused by a sensory overload
    c. A feeling of discomfort due to contradictory information
    d. A lack of compatibility between instruction and learning

94. Which of these is NOT a pair of low-impact teacher interventions that prevent undesirable student behaviors from escalating?
    a. Showing interest in student work and encouraging students in their endeavors
    b. Showing awareness of student behaviors through physical proximity and touch
    c. Embarrassing and punishing students in front of classmates to prevent rebellion
    d. Reminding students of successful instances and modifying lesson presentations

95. Of the following, which is a principle wherein Albert Bandura's theory *agrees with* behaviorist learning theory?
    a. Consequences reinforce or punish behaviors.
    b. Learning always results in a change in behavior.
    c. Internal cognitive processes must be examined.
    d. Social interactions are very important in learning.

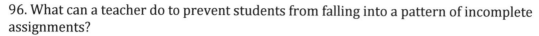

96. What can a teacher do to prevent students from falling into a pattern of incomplete assignments?

    a. Ask the students to keep an eye on each other and report to you if someone else is having a problem.
    b. Increase the penalty for not finishing assignments
    c. Approach a student privately the first time the student fails to turn in an assignment and let the student know you are available to help
    d. Assign extra credit work to students who fail to turn in assignments

97. Which of the following actions is most likely to be considered "fair use" under U.S. copyright law?

    a. Printing out a copy of an e-book for a student who cannot afford to purchase the book
    b. Copying several chapters out of a textbook for a student who lost his textbook
    c. Copying the assigned homework questions from a textbook for a student who was home sick for a few days
    d. Borrowing a DVD movie from the library and making a copy to show to students each year

98. During in-class assignments and small group activities, how can a teacher best ensure that all of the students are on-task and not getting behind?

    a. Watch the class quietly from the teacher's desk
    b. Respond to students promptly when they raise their hands
    c. Collect all student work several times during the class, check it, and then hand it back so that they can continue working
    d. Circulate among the students regularly to observe the students' work up close

99. Mrs. Cranston, a seventh grade science teacher, tries to provide her students with several options when assigning projects. This approach is useful because it fosters emotional development in which of the following areas?

    a. Development of a variety of learning approaches
    b. Development of self-concept
    c. Developing a sense of autonomy
    d. Developing identification with peer groups

100. In scaffolded instruction, what is the correct sequence (first to last) of these steps?

    a. Teacher modeling, student think-alouds; student-teacher collaboration; student paired/small-group work, scaffolded as needed; independent student practice
    b. Independent student practice; student-teacher collaboration; teacher modeling, student think-alouds; student paired/small-group work, scaffolded as needed
    c. Student-teacher collaboration; student paired/small-group work, scaffolded as needed; independent student practice; teacher modeling, student think-alouds
    d. Student paired/small-group work, scaffolded as needed; teacher modeling, student think-alouds; independent student practice; student-teacher collaboration

18

101. Room arrangement is part of classroom management. Which one of the following is *not* true about appropriate arrangements?

    a. Students don't necessarily need to see the teacher, but do need to see the blackboard, poster, or whatever demonstrates the lesson.
    b. Desks should be arranged such that the teacher can get close to every student.
    c. Desks or tables should be arranged to fit the activity; for example, small group discussion or independent work.
    d. Teachers should select who sits where and by whom.

102. Among legal rights and responsibilities of students, which of these is federal rather than varying by state or district?

    a. Free, appropriate public education
    b. Reporting dangerous behaviors
    c. Advocating for policy changes
    d. Peaceful dispute resolution

103. What is the most efficient way to apply a formula for determining final grades?

    a. Paper, pencil, and a calculator
    b. Database manager software
    c. Spreadsheet software
    d. Online resources

104. A fifth grade science teacher has used a new textbook this year, and she wants to evaluate its effectiveness compared with that of the textbook she used in previous years. Which of the following strategies would be most appropriate?

    a. Comparing this year's students' performance on standardized tests to the standardized test scores of the students she taught in previous years using the old book
    b. Comparing this year's students' performance on norm-referenced in-class tests to the test scores of the students she taught in previous years using the old book
    c. Comparing current students' improvement on a criterion-referenced test administered at the beginning and the end of the year to previous students' improvement on that same test throughout the year
    d. Surveying current students' interest in science and comparing it to previous students' interest in science

105. During her annual review, Mr. Ainsley is told by the school principal that his teaching is good overall, but that his portfolio shows that he does not assess his students as often or as effectively as he should. What actions should Mr. Ainsley take first to correct this problem?

    a. Write a letter to the principal stating that he thinks this assessment of his teaching is unfair, and explaining his reasons for his failure to assess his students adequately
    b. Use available professional development resources on assessment to develop a plan to improve his use of assessment in the classroom and present it to the principal for review
    c. Confer with other teachers to find out if the principal made similar suggestions to them about improving their assessment techniques
    d. Sign up for an assessment workshop that will occur in a few months and let the principal know that he will need to take a few days off work to attend the workshop

106. According to the U.S. Department of Education (ED), at which of these levels is a teacher not a student teacher, but paid, and not a teacher of record, but completing a supervised practicum?

a. Novice Teacher
b. Leader Teacher
c. Master Teacher
d. Resident Teacher

107. Legal blindness is defined as which of the following visual acuity measures on an eye test?

a. 20/200
b. 20/70
c. 10/200
d. 5/200

108. For how long at a time should a teacher initially plan to hold open class discussions of subject matter at the middle school/junior high school level?

a. 3-5 minutes
b. 10-15 minutes
c. 30-45 minutes
d. For an entire class period

109. According to experts, how should teachers distribute the cognitive levels of the questions they ask relative to student grade levels?

a. All elementary and secondary grades should be asked half higher- and half lower-level questions.
b. More than half the questions should be at higher cognitive levels for all student grades.
c. More than half at higher levels for secondary grades, below half in elementary grades.
d. More than half the questions should be at lower cognitive levels for all student grades.

110. When presenting information, effective teacher communication is best achieved when the teacher uses which of the following types of phrases?

a. because, for example
b. not many, not very
c. somewhere, somehow
d. generally, usually

111. Which approach to assessment offers the strongest chance of quantifying what a student has learned?

a. Multiple choice tests
b. Essay questions
c. Combining several methods
d. Tests using a simple question-and-answer format

112. What is correct about FERPA regulations regarding school disclosure of student "directory" information?

a. Schools must obtain written consent of the student's parents prior to disclosure.
b. Schools can disclose names, addresses, and birth dates, but not phone numbers.
c. Schools must notify parents and students of FERPA rights, but must not disclose.
d. Schools can disclose, but with enough prior notice for requesting non-disclosure.

113. Which of the following describes the process of inductive reasoning?

    a. Top-down and general to specific
    b. Bottom-up and general to specific
    c. Bottom-up and specific to general
    d. Top-down and specific to general

114. A teacher wanting to show items from various cultures to the children in her classroom asks a child of Chinese heritage to bring a coolie hat to school. The family is insulted by the teacher's assumption that all Chinese are/were coolies. What is the best response for the teacher once she has realized her mistake?

    a. Apologize and let the issue drop.
    b. Rescind the request to other families for cultural items to avoid more problems.
    c. Ask the family to send whatever it feels appropriate.
    d. Have the child make a coolie hat in class since one was not available at home.

115. To communicate high expectations to all students, what should teachers do?

    a. Identify which students they expect less from as early as they can.
    b. Avoid identifying student similarities that influence expectations.
    c. Realize teacher expectations have more influence than behaviors.
    d. Treat students differently according to what they expect of them.

116. Students who are English Language Learners usually have which of the following traits in common?

    a. A need for special education services
    b. Normal to above-average intelligence
    c. Above-average academic performance
    d. Below-average academic aptitude due to their cultural background

117. According to Jean Piaget's four-stage theory of cognitive development, the distinction between people at the concrete operational stage (approximately 7-12 years of age) and the formal operational stage (approximately 12-16 years of age) of development is that:

    a. Unlike those at the concrete operational stage, those at the formal operational stage can think logically in concrete terms
    b. Unlike those at the concrete operational stage, those at the formal operational stage are highly reliant on sensory and motor skills to learn
    c. Those in the concrete operational stage are capable of abstract thought, while those at the formal operational stage can think only in concrete terms
    d. Those in the concrete operational stage can think logically only with respect to concrete experiences, while those at the formal operational stage can reason in abstract and hypothetical terms

118. In what areas do computers consistently demonstrate the greatest benefit in the classroom?

    a. Simple drills presented, such as teaching multiplication tables. This frees up the teacher to work with the students on developing higher-level skills.
    b. Role-playing games that develop greater social awareness, and allow the students to participate more directly in the events they are learning about.
    c. Simulations of mechanical activities that help the student's develop motor skills and reflexes.
    d. Exercises that teach higher-order thinking and professional skills.

119. Several of Ms. Holloway's students are in foster care. One student is constantly being shifted among different foster parents, and the students' academic performance is suffering considerably since he went into foster care. Which of the following would be the most appropriate way for Ms. Holloway to respond to this problem?

a. She should ignore the problem for the time being, since the student is simply distracted by his unstable home environment and will be able to catch up once he returns to his family
b. She should contact the student's current foster parents to inform them of the problem so they can help the student with math
c. She should contact the student's social services caseworker about the problem so that he or she can inform each of the students' successive foster parents of the importance of helping the student with math
d. She should give the student easier math assignments until the student returns home so that his grades will not suffer

120. Strategies for establishing a verbal-linguistic learning environment include all except which one of the following?

a. Classroom discussions
b. Stories told by the teacher
c. Task Cards
d. Word walls

121. Which method is the most helpful in making sure that students understand their progress throughout the term?

a. In addition to your own records, require that each student keep a grade book for him or herself
b. Once a week, read each student's current average out loud to the class
c. Have students check their own work
d. Issue an informal written progress report every two weeks

122. According to the provisions of FERPA, when can schools furnish student records without consent?

a. To some doing studies, if on behalf of the school.
b. Court orders and legal subpoenas are insufficient.
c. Safety or health emergencies still require consent.
d. To juvenile justice system authorities in all states.

123. What is correct about the definition of independent study as an instructional strategy?

a. It involves only an individual student working alone.
b. It can include individuals, partners, or small groups.
c. It can involve paired students but not small groups.
d. It can involve small groups but not paired students.

124. Suppose the students in your computer science class vary greatly in the amount of experience and knowledge they have about computers. What can you do as a teacher to make student evaluations fair to everyone?

    a. Evaluate how much each student learns in addition to whether or not the student gets the correct answers on tests
    b. Grade class tests on a curve
    c. Put more weight on class research projects than on tests
    d. Grade students only according to test results

125. In independent instruction, what is included in student research projects?

    a. Teachers assign research questions for students to investigate.
    b. Students develop research questions; teachers supply sources.
    c. Teachers provide guidance to students only as they require this.
    d. Students must communicate their results without any guidance.

126. Which of the following is an advantage of using anecdotal notes to assess student work?

    a. Teachers can use these to collect information both during assessment and outside of it.
    b. Unless a teacher adds norms or criteria for comparison, these notes lack standardization.
    c. Teachers cannot record observations of individual student behaviors as with most tools.
    d. Writing anecdotal notes can yield valuable insights but often lack any supporting context.

127. How should teachers arrange classroom furnishings and materials to create supportive climates?

    a. Arrangements should not let students feel too comfortable.
    b. Arrangements should discourage dialogue among students.
    c. Arrangements should keep students from owning the room.
    d. Arrangements should support collaboration among students.

128. Mr. Swanson has implemented a token economy behavior management system for several disruptive students in his class. For each day that the students exhibit appropriate behavior, they earn a check mark, and if they have earned three check marks by the end of the week, they are allowed to play computer games for 30 minutes on Friday afternoon. So far, all of the students have earned enough check marks each week to get the reward, but each student is still disrupting class at least once per week. Which of the following strategies would probably be most effective for further reducing the students' disruptive behavior?

    a. Taking away a check mark that the student has already earned if they engage in disruptive behavior
    b. Explaining to the students that they have done a good job of improving their behavior, but that they can do even better; as a consequence, they now need to earn four check marks to get the reward, which is 45 minutes on the computer
    c. Increasing the reward to one hour of computer time
    d. Implementing a system where students start out with five check marks at the beginning of the week, and lose one check mark for each episode of disruptive behavior; students who still have five check marks at the end of the week earn 30 minutes of computer time

129. Which of the following is consistent with constructive assertiveness on the part of a teacher?

a. Telling students in a literature class that there is only one acceptable point of view in regard to the novel you are teaching

b. A teacher who asks permission from her students to begin class

c. A teacher who halts his presentation and sternly insists that the students in the back of the room stop talking

d. A teacher who yells at students who answer questions incorrectly

130. Teachers can positively communicate expectations in such a way as to make students eager to learn. Of the following statements, which one would be the least effective?

a. "We're going to think like scientists in this class."

b. "You might not like this practice, but it will help you to get a good grade."

c. "I know you are all curious about how to make a puppet."

d. "This project is one of my hobbies, so I wanted to share it with you."

Answer Key and Explanation

1. B: Spina bifida is the condition of incomplete closure of the neural tube in the spinal column. As such, it affects the spinal nerves and commonly causes paresis (paralysis) or weakness in the lower body. Motor dyspraxia or apraxia (a), i.e., damage to the parts of the brain's cerebrum that control and coordinate muscular movements; athetosis (c), i.e., involuntary, uncontrolled body movements; and spasticity (d), i.e., excessive muscular rigidity and tension, are all common symptoms of cerebral palsy, a condition caused by damage to the brain, not the spinal cord.

2. B: The first step that Mr. Copeland should take is to try to create a tutoring program in which older students and literate parents volunteer to provide homework support after school or during lunch. While guiding parents to community resources that can help them improve their reading skills would also be helpful (A), it would still take a significant amount of time for these parents to develop their skills to the level at which they could comfortably help their students with reading homework.

3. D: Middle school is a critical time during which students develop a tolerance of diversity, make the decision to continue with school, and tolerance for those who are different. Middle school students also develop higher-order thinking skills, but this represents cognitive development, rather than value development.

4. B: This creates a temptation for some of the students to dishonestly change their grades. Answer A works well, but does require more time from the teacher. Answer C is a very efficient method for recording grades in this situation, although it does require sacrificing a little bit of class time. Answer D is ideal, although not all teachers have a teacher's aide to rely on.

5. B: In its model for involving parents via parent-educator partnership for enhancing student achievement, ED includes both communicating accountability data in a timely way and communicating teacher qualifications (a) in core subjects; training parents both to help their children achieve academically and to influence school policy (b) through participation in school advisory councils and other groups; equally emphasizing both opportunities for home and school involvement and also supplemental education services (c) available; and communicating in whichever languages and formats are appropriate (d) for individual parents.

6. A: Conflict resolution experts advise teachers, based on research results, to instruct students in good listening behaviors, including asking questions as needed but not interrupting others; making eye contact (b) with others while listening to them; avoiding giving others suggestions or advice about what they shared (c); and providing speakers with positive reinforcement by nodding and smiling (d) while listening when appropriate.

7. A: Extended practice should be part of the lesson when the teacher's evaluation shows that extended practice is needed to solidify the lesson or ensure that all students have learned the objective. The closing of the lesson is too late to try to back up and insert extended practice. When closing a lesson, it is natural to review key points, perhaps as demonstrated by work done by the students during the lesson, and giving the students a preview of the next or other related lessons builds student anticipation and desire to learn.

8. A: Conducting interviews is a strategy best used for verbal-linguistic students who use speaking, such as asking questions of another person, to learn. Students who are dominantly logical-mathematical learners will learn best in the areas of mathematics, science, and logic. Strategies in these areas include using Venn diagrams to logically illustrate relationships; thinking in probabilities, which emphasizes working with numbers; and discerning patterns, which is a mathematical thinking process.

9. C: If Mrs. Frances wants to develop a theme-based unit that is interesting and relevant to her fifth grade students, the best approach would be to conduct an informal, open-ended survey to look for interests that her students share. This approach would allow Mrs. Frances to find a topic that would interest the broadest range of students. While presenting several topics for students to vote upon (D) would also come close to achieving this goal, it is a less desirable alternative because it artificially narrows the choices available to students by predetermining the options.

10. B: By breaking the class up into more homogenous groups you can more easily address the needs of all the students. Keep in mind that this works better in some subject areas than in it does in others. Answer A is what many teachers do, but it leaves out the needs of the strongest and weakest students. Answer C is not very practical, since you will likely be working with the weaker students every day after class, and will not have much time when the stronger students need help. Answer D would be ideal in a perfect world, but it is very likely that one of the reasons that your class is so heterogeneous is that there may not be remedial or advanced classes available, or that the weakest and strongest students in your class fell to the cracks between these classes.

11. B: Cooperative learning exercises (working in small groups) teach students how to solve problems in groups. These skills are essential to success in many jobs. Answer A is the opposite of cooperative learning. Answers C and D are unrelated to the topic of the question.

12. A: According to research findings, teacher learning environment strategies that produce high student engagement and low student misbehavior include focusing on the whole class when alerting student attention (a); communicating teacher awareness of student behaviors to students (b); designing and implementing overlapping activities (c); and lesson planning and delivery that enable instructional momentum (d).

13. B: The fact that rubrics combine learning objectives, tasks, guidance to students for performing those tasks, and criteria (a) for evaluating student task performance is an advantage they have as assessment tools. The fact that the performance levels they assign are not as precise as number or letter grades or percentages (b) is a disadvantage. The fact that they are brief in nature (c) is an advantage for both students and teachers. The fact that they are both more concise and clearer than many other assessment tools (d) is another advantage.

14. A: This is a specific, practical that can be taught, tested, and evaluated. Answer B is ambiguous, and it cannot be effectively evaluated. Answer C sounds specific, but in fact deals in opinion. What makes a poem good is a subjective matter about which people disagree. Answer D is also ambiguous. The learning goals for each unit should be specific and measurable.

15. D: Research finds that teacher practices and school policies are more predictive of how involved parents will be in their children's educations than the parents' race or ethnicity (a), the marital status of the parents (b), or the parents' own levels of education (c) are.

16. D: In order to assess the effectiveness of the team-teaching model, the teachers should compare their sixth grade students' performance this year with the performance of students in previous years where team teaching was not used. This will eliminate the possibility of differences among schools that would be present if they compared their students to students in other schools (C). It would also rule out the possibility that performance typically increases in sixth grade relative to previous years, which would be present if they only compared the students' performance this year

26

to their performance in previous year. They should also consider the performance history of this particular group of sixth graders relative to previous groups to rule out the possibility that this group of students' performance has been higher or lower overall.

17. D: Mr. Mailer should explain to the parents that the decision is ultimately theirs, but also provide them with educational resources about reading disabilities and emphasize that delaying receipt of special education services can exacerbate the problems associated with reading disabilities. Teachers cannot have students formally tested for learning disabilities without their parents' permission, but it is Mr. Mailer's professional responsibility to advocate for his student and explain to Thomas' parents the possible consequences of their decision to delay testing.

18. A: It is the teacher's responsibility to observe and verify that students are following the instructions and participating equally. Answer B is likely to produce biased results. Answer C defeats the purpose of the exercise. The point is for the students to learn how to effectively divide group tasks on their own. Answer D simply denies students the experience of learning this valuable lesson.

19. B: In order to begin resolving the problem, Ms. Mattingly should first confer with her principal and other fourth grade teachers to determine whether her grade level expectations for academic achievement align with those of the district as a whole. Since she was previously unaware of the fact that her students were falling behind, the most logical explanation for this situation is that her academic expectations for her students are not as high as those used by school administrators in constructing the test. She should definitely not ignore the standardized test results (A) or ask the students' parents to resolve the problem themselves (D). She may not need to change her instructional methods either (C), if the problem is simply that her expectations are too low.

20. A: Computer-monitored drills have only limited use in the classroom for short periods of time. Otherwise, students become quickly bored and do not learn. Teachers should not rely on computers to do the "grunt work" of teaching. Teachers should be as deeply involved as the students during sessions of computer-oriented teaching.

21. D: The teacher who speaks softly and avoids making eye contact with students is less likely to command respect and obedience in the classroom. All three of the other answers represent assertive body language that is more likely to result in students responding well to the teacher. This includes looking students in the eye, speaking in a firm voice, and maintaining good posture.

22. B: Using additional visual aids and hand gestures will help get your points across more clearly. Answer A is inappropriate. The parents should not have to pay for a translator, and such a strategy would also not encourage the student to increase her English skills. Answer C would make it even harder for the student to understand. Answer D would be unfair to the other students, since it would greatly slow down you class and make it impossible to you to cover your material on schedule.

23. C: The libido is part of the id according to Freud. It represents psychic energy as well as sex drive. Freud's three major personality structures are the id (a), which generates unconscious impulses; the ego (b), which realistically regulates acting on id impulses; and the superego (c), which morally regulates the id and ego.

24. B: This will bring the story into a modern context, making it easier to understand. Having them search for differences will ensure that they actually read the original as well. Answer A would certainly be helpful, but by itself is not likely to prevent students from losing interest. Answer C is also a useful practice, but without a real understanding of the context, much of the drama will be lost upon the students. Answer D will almost certainly put most of the students to sleep, and is unnecessary for studying a single play.

25. C: Mr. Robinson can achieve this objective using a theme-based unit. Theme-based units allow students to explore a topic of interest from many different perspectives, and use their reading, math, writing and reasoning skills to learn more about the topic. For example, in a theme-based unit about weather, students might learn how to use number lines by reading a thermometer, read about the devastating effects of severe weather, and write about a time that the weather affected their lives.

26. D: The most effective way for Mrs. Alito to meet the student's needs without making him feel uncomfortable or disrupting the rest of her class would be to keep an eye on the student and provide him with a nonverbal signal that he can use if he wants to go to the resource room. This would prevent him from disrupting the class and drawing attention to himself by asking to leave (B) or doing relaxation exercises (C). Answer A (checking in on the student every few hours) would not be effective because it would not be sufficiently responsive to the student's needs.

27. B: Frequent evaluations show how students perform on a weekly or daily basis. Moreover, they often reveal problems earlier enough that they can be effectively address without ruining the student's grades. Answer A is not always reliable since a student may be nervous or not functioning at his/her best on the particular day of the test. Answer C is nonsense. A teacher's evaluation should always be based on objective indicators. Answer D can certainly be useful, but these assignments do not indicate how a student performs under controlled conditions and without access to references such as calculators, encyclopedias, or help from family members.

28. D: Mr. Ivanov should find someone to help him write a note to the parents in Spanish explaining that he will help them find a volunteer translator if they do not have a friend or family member who could translate for them. Since parent-teacher communication is very important to students' development, Mr. Ivanov should make every reasonable effort to ensure that the parents can participate in conferences. Simply telling the parents or his principal to find a translator would create an unnecessary barrier to the parents' participation in the conferences. Asking fifth-graders to serve as translators for their own parent-teacher conferences would be inappropriate since students of this age are not usually present during these conferences, and their presence could prevent a frank discussion between the teacher and the parents from occurring.

29. B: Strategies for effective parent-teacher conferences based on teacher experience include beginning each conference with something positive about the student before addressing improvements needed (a); sandwiching every criticism between two positives (b); sending parents conference invitations with forms for parents to write and return their questions and concerns in advance, and lists of major topics and teacher expectations for parents to read (c) to help parents prepare for conference collaborations on plans for students; and having student work samples ready (d) to discuss with parents.

30. C: In a highly diversified class, teachers often fall into the trap of offering too much encouragement to the strongest students while neglecting the weaker students. As a result, the weaker students become resentful and feel little incentive to work harder. Answer A is not a mistake. The weaker students need more of the teacher's attention. Answer B is not really a problem as long as the stronger students are respectful and provide accurate information. Answer D is, again, not really a mistake. The weaker students need to be corrected in order to learn. Of course, the teacher should take care not to make the students feel bad about themselves.

31. A: In order to send Ellen electronic copies of paper worksheets, a scanner and email, a disc or flash drive would probably be needed, but a copy machine would not be necessary. The teachers could scan the documents using a scanner and send them as an email attachment or save them to a disc. The disc could then be sent home and Ellen could download the documents and print them out, or Ellen could open and print the email attachment.

32. B: When a teacher is consistent in how she runs her classroom, the students will more quickly understand the rules, and will also recognize that the rules apply equally to everyone. Answer A can work in some classrooms, but some students will find this to be too intense. Answer C will lead to the students taking advantage of the teacher and misbehaving even more. Answer D will likely lead to chaos. While it wise not to let the students "get a rise out of you," the teacher should always react so that it will be clear that misbehavior is not tolerated.

33. C: Many new teachers make the mistake of getting so caught up in their lesson that they fail to notice problem behavior in the classroom before it gets out of hand. Teachers must learn to divide their attention between all aspects of the class environment, and to periodically scan the room and take account of what is going on. Like juggling, this is a skill that takes time and practice to develop. All new teachers must work hard to become competent at it.

34. C: Introducing new material using several different strategies will help make it more accessible to a larger group of students, regardless of their specific backgrounds. All three of the other answers represent a shallow approach to diversity that presumes that different cultures adhere to stereotypes. The truth is that different students think differently, and using a wider variety of teaching methods will cast a wider net.

35. B: Research has determined that family involvement in education improves all of these: student self-esteem, student attitudes (a), student attendance, student behavior (c), and student test scores, grades, and rates of post-secondary school (d) enrollment.

36. A: ED identifies Professional Teachers as tenured teachers who coach and advocate academically, serve as examples of lifelong learning, and often stay at this level throughout their teaching careers. ED identifies Resident Teachers (b) as paid teachers, but not teachers of record and not student teachers, who are completing their supervised residency or practicum required for certification. ED identifies Master Teachers (c) as school team leaders, classroom teachers, faculty support providers, and professional team teaching resources and models, and further identifies Teacher Leaders (d) as combining leadership and teaching, designing review/evaluation systems, and developing practice communities.

37. C: The philosophy and psychology of actively constructing one's own knowledge of the world is known as constructivism. Scaffolding (a) is temporary needed support teachers provide for student learning and gradually withdraw as students acquire higher skill levels. Cognitivism (b) is the type of psychology Piaget's theory involves as a theory of cognitive development; however, the description of actively building one's own knowledge refers specifically to constructivism. The Zone of Proximal Development (d) was Vygotsky's term for the distance between what a learner can do independently and what that learner can do with help or guidance.

38. C: Central auditory processing disorder is categorized as an auditory disability because it impairs the ability to understand spoken language received through the auditory sense (hearing). But it does not involve the outer, middle, or inner ear or auditory nerves. It involves a deficit in the brain's ability to interpret the meanings and structures of speech sounds. Sensorineural hearing loss (a) involves the cochlea in the inner ear and/or auditory nerves leading to the brain.

Conductive hearing loss (b) involves the outer and/or middle ear, where something obstructs conduction of sound, e.g., a deformed pinna/auricle, wax buildup, a closed or malformed or ear canal, fluid/pus buildup in the middle ear due to otitis media (middle ear infection), otosclerosis immobilizing the ossicles in the middle ear, etc. Complete deafness (d) most typically involves total sensorineural hearing loss.

39. B: While students love getting out of the classroom, this is not the only benefit of field trips (a): they let students apply knowledge and skills learned in the classroom to real life. Rather than confusing students (c), real-world variations inform them how reality differs from academic conditions. For example, rock samples in school geology labs typically have equal distribution, but in the real world quartz is more abundant; lab samples are often pure, but in the field rocks/minerals are more often mixed. Interaction with nature is a benefit *along with* real, hands-on learning (d).

40. C: Large projects should receive several grades, and students tend to be more motivated if the teacher grades them as the project moves along. Answer A might be appropriate for seniors, but otherwise, students of this age are not organized enough to handle that level of responsibility. Answer B has little to do with the overall grading strategy. Answer D tends to punish students who make extra effort, since they get nothing for it in return. Instead it encourages students to only do what is absolutely necessary to meet the criteria.

41. D: Indirect instruction promotes student exploration, inquiry, discovery learning, problem solving, and learning abstract concepts and patterns. It is delivered implicitly, whereas direct instruction is delivered explicitly (a). Lesson plans vary, whereas direct instruction uses uniform lesson plans (b). It is less structured, whereas direct instruction is more structured (c). Direct instruction promotes piquing initial student interest; learning facts, rules, and sequences; and analyzing text/workbook material. Whereas indirect instruction is student-centered, direct instruction is teacher-centered.

42. D: Students with specific learning disabilities (SLDs) do not have intellectual impairments; they have impairments in processing information. Therefore it is most typical of students with SLDs to show a marked gap between intellectual ability and school performance. Students with ASDs (a) can have any degree of intellectual impairment or none. Those with high IQs may excel academically but have difficulty with social interactions, transitions, and sensory input, and/or demonstrate rigid routines and schedules, restricted interests, and repetitive behaviors. Students with ID (b) typically learn the same ways as others, but more slowly. Generally their intellectual ability and school performance are less disparate than those of students with SLDs. Hence (c) is incorrect.

43. C: Teacher behaviors that promote school-home communication include devoting equal time to listening to parents/families (a), mutually exchanging teacher and family expertise (b) with each other, and brainstorming with families to find strategies supporting individual students (d). However, when teachers limit their behaviors with families to telling them what to do (c), this impedes school-home communication.

44. C: Students in low-income schools may have poor perceptions of their academic ability, but extensive research shows that this disadvantage can be overcome with effective instruction and high expectations. While additional resources (D) may be helpful in providing more effective instruction, they are neither necessary for nor a guarantee of academic improvement.

45. A: Building rapport with parents at the beginning of the school year is a teacher strategy inviting parental involvement and partnership by showing that teachers value the importance of parental contributions, rather than only contacting/meeting with parents about problems (b). Rather than avoid all advice, teachers should offer all families information for positive home learning environments (c), e.g., homework spaces, homework-checking plans, scheduling homework, limiting TV, etc. While some topics are private, teachers usually should ask families (d) about expectations for students, current homework support, emotional impacts of hardships, student home responsibilities, and how teachers and schools can help.

46. D: Teachers should apply common sense in this decision, and consider the needs of their class as appropriate. Answers A and B both represent closed-minded approaches to the question. Word processors are a part of modern life and employment, and it is completely appropriate for students to learn the use of these programs since they will likely need to know how to use them later in life. Obviously, it does not make sense for students to have access to a word processor during a spelling test. Answer C is illogical. After all, students are asked to use commercial products in their schoolwork all the time, including their own textbooks.

47. D: Reviewing the students' notes will quickly identify anyone who lacks good note-taking skills. Depending upon how many students are having trouble, you can then either devote some class time to a discussion of note-taking or meet with students individually. Answer A is not a solution. As a teacher preparing children for college, it is your responsibility to ensure that they have skills such as these. Answer B would seriously interrupt the flow of your lesson plan, while at the same time it would not necessarily test the students note taking, but rather their general recollection ability. Answer C wastes valuable class time and does not allow the teacher to verify that students actually develop their note-taking skills.

48. B: When children engage in "pretend" or "make-believe" playing, as when they play "house" and pretend to be parents; pretend to be fantasy characters; or use toys to represent real persons, animals, machines, etc., they understand one thing can be used as a symbol to stand for something else, i.e., symbolic representation. When babies look for things they saw that were then hidden so they can no longer see them (A), they have attained object permanence. The emergence of this understanding that things out of sight still exist is also indicated by their enjoying playing "peek-a-boo" (C). (Infants without object permanence are truly surprised to see a hidden face reappear; those developing object permanence laugh with delight to see the face reappear; and those with fully developed object permanence may eventually lose interest in the game.) When children can add or subtract using pennies (D) or other concrete objects, this shows they have attained concrete operations, i.e., mental operations using concrete objects.

49. D: To encourage student development of intrinsic motivation, teachers can interest students in learning content by having a strong interest in it themselves (a); demonstrating their own interest in the content to students (b); getting to know students and their individual interests (c); and moreover, connecting learning content to those student interests (d).

50. A: Teachers who are aware of individual students' group roles as a part of group dynamics apply their understanding to manage their classrooms by developing friendly relationships with students who play roles in groups of leaders, instigators, and consciences; they also do this by developing strategies for keeping students who play group roles of procurers and negotiators on-task (c) rather than developing friendly relationships with them (b), and rather than by applying both strategies equally with students in all roles (d).

51. B: Planning requires abstract thinking (a), as it involves mentally representing actions before actually performing them, and imagination (b) to envision doing things not done yet. Planning both requires and promotes organization as well as imagination (c). Planning is identified as being on a higher level among higher-order thinking skills, not lower (d).

52. B: Research-based strategies found to promote student motivation include not only teacher interest in student learning, but also teacher personal interest (a) in their students' backgrounds and concerns; teacher demonstration of their own motivation and passion as role models for students (b); teacher belief in students' abilities (c) as well as interest in students; and teacher personalization of content for individual students (d).

53. B: Lesson objectives should have an important outcome, should be useful to the students in the future, and should be at a knowledge and skill level appropriate to the students; however, activities should be planned to fit the objective, not the other way around. Every lesson plan should be concerned with an important learning outcome - trivial lessons are a waste of time and damage student interest – therefore, all lesson plans should include an important objective. The knowledge gained by a lesson should also be something students can use in the future; otherwise the lesson has no point. The lesson should also be comprehensible to the students – teaching above their skill levels leaves them unsuccessful and frustrated; teaching below their skills levels leaves them bored.

54. D: When you punish him in front of the class, he probably wants to show the other students that he is not afraid of you. If you speak to him in private, you may find that he is more reasonable, and more willing to tell you what the problem really is. Jethro's behavior is typical of an adolescent who comes from an impoverished neighborhood. He grew up knowing that he must always be on the defensive and that losing face often means losing your life. He learned a long time ago that you must never appear weak, even to adults. He also probably feels that he must prove to the other students that "they are no better than he is" just because they have more money.

55. B: The approach of the teacher's "simple authority statement" authoritatively stops student misbehavior with a minimum of emotional distress (a); models reasonable, respectful use of authority for students (b); and expresses teacher disapproval of student behavior as objectively as possible (c), and does so immediately (d).

56. C: Using analytical checklists as assessment tools has the advantage of saving time and effort by listing the tasks, skills, or behaviors to be performed and assessed in advance. They also have the advantage of making assessment uniform across students relative to tasks and/or their components (a). They do require additional notes for teachers to identify other notable feats that teachers observe students accomplishing beyond the designated tasks (b), but this is a disadvantage. Although some checklists include performance levels similarly to rubrics, others constrain assessment to Yes/No responses (d), another disadvantage.

57. C: Teachers can stimulate active student involvement in subject content by asking both cognitively lower-level questions requiring students to remember and understand information, and cognitively higher-level questions requiring students to apply, analyze, evaluate, and/or synthesize information rather than only the former (a) or only the latter (b). Even simple factual questions engage students by requiring them to think about and respond to them. Therefore, it is not true that questions will not promote active student involvement (d).

58. A: Child custody arrangements between divorced parents can complicate how available each or both parents are to participate in their children's education. Additional factors that often make it more difficult for parents to participate include parent work schedules (b), lack of transportation (c), and the number of children in the family (d).

59. D: Because inclusive education is a federal legal mandate and mainstreaming is the commonest means of compliance today, regular classroom teachers most often have the responsibility for the instruction of special-needs students—even if these students are also assigned educational specialists (a), special education teachers (b), and whichever therapists are most applicable (c) to an individual student's needs. Classroom teachers collaborate with these personnel, but still usually have the main responsibility for instruction.

60. D: Ms. Swanson should explain to the parent that her daughter has missed several homework assignments, and offer to tell the parent about future assignments so that she can ensure that her daughter completes them. This answer is better than answer B, because it lays out a clear plan for correcting the problem. Answer C is not correct because teachers are permitted to discuss students' academic records with the students' parents as long as those students are under the age of 18. Answer A is also incorrect because failure to turn in homework assignments does not necessarily indicate that a student doesn't understand the course content. Other causes of the problem should be eliminated before academic remediation is pursued.

61. A: the teacher's most important responsibility is to create an accepting, non-judgmental classroom environment. Since homeless students attending school face many obstacles ranging from transience to lack of appropriate clothing and hygiene tools, they will be more likely to continue attending if they are accepted by their teachers and peers. Since the student is living in a shelter, the relevant social service agency is responsible for ensuring that the student is fed and clothed. Teachers are also not responsible for diagnosing mental illnesses, although the teacher should inform the student's parent or caseworker know if she suspects a problem. While the teacher may want to screen the student for possible learning disabilities, she should not assume that poor academic performance is the result of a disability. Homelessness often results in prolonged absence from school and emotional problems that interfere with learning, and these factors may explain poor performance.

62. C: The teacher should first discuss the problem with the special education teacher, who may have additional insight on the problem based on information in the student's Individualized Education Plan (IEP). Adjustments to the IEP may be necessary if current strategies are ineffective. The student's parents should also be notified about the problem, but the special education teacher should be informed about any problems first. Punishing a student with a behavioral disability through isolation or any other method must be done after discussions with the special education teacher in order to be effective, and may actually constitute discrimination if not implemented appropriately.

63. C: The ability to learn languages with relative ease is a characteristic of the verbal-linguistic learner. Teachers discern the learning styles of students through testing or observation. A student who likes field trips and physical exercise is likely a tactile-kinesthetic learner who enjoys the physical activity of a field trip or any physical exercise because such a student learns through involvement of the body. Similarly, a tactile-kinesthetic learner will exhibit greater skill with balance and dexterity. A student who is good at logical problem solving is likely a logical-mathematical learner.

64. C: Following current events is a great way to show the students how the work of Congress affects their everyday lives. Holding in-class discussions will reveal areas where the students' knowledge is weak, and will make your explanations more interesting. Answer D illustrates a useful tool, but charts and graphs alone will not motivate your students. Answer B does represent a way to get the students more actively involved in the subject, but learning the biographies of senators will not help the students to understand the overall structure and function of Congress. Answer A is quite simply an ineffective way to make students learn.

65. B: The major educational benefit of using class discussion is that it allows students to explore the subtleties of learning objectives by considering them in various contexts and from various social, cultural and historical perspectives. This is an important aspect of the development of higher-order thinking skills.

66. B: The occupational therapist is most qualified to inform classroom teachers of activities that develop student fine motor skills and skills for completing activities of daily living (ADL). The physical therapist (a) is more qualified to inform teachers of exercises and activities that develop gross motor skills, and to make and adapt assistive devices. The special education teacher (c) is more qualified to help classroom teachers adapt/modify curriculum and instruction for special student needs and provide strategies for inclusive and differentiated instruction. The OT's specific expertise is not equally available from any other IEP team members (d).

67. D: Grades 2-12 students at the Intermediate level as having limited writing ability, so even readers familiar with ELL writing may only partially understand what they write. In reading, they comprehend connected *simple* sentences about *familiar* subjects (a). They can communicate ideas in writing about *familiar, concrete* topics (b). They frequently read text in *short phrases, slowly, with* rereading as needed for clarification (c).

68. B: When teachers use performance continua for assessment, they can describe student performance evaluatively with more precision than when they assign separate grades (a), an advantage. However, for comparing assessment scores among students, classes, and/or schools, the lack of exact numbers on a continuum is a disadvantage (b). On the other hand, the performance ranges provided by continua are more realistic and accurate than assigning exact numerical scores or referring to cutoff scores (c), an advantage. Except for comparisons (b)—in which case standardized tests are better—the superiority of continua for individualized assessment (d) is an advantage.

69. D: Para-educators are not permitted to perform only concrete services (a); they also assist classroom teachers with instructing students, grading tests and papers, etc. They do not typically work as volunteers (b); though some volunteers may perform paraprofessional jobs, many are hired and paid by schools. While their duties may include performing tasks for therapists, e.g., observing students and collecting behavioral data, they must first be trained (c) by the therapists they assist. Para-educators can often help teachers by working one-on-one with individual students (d).

70. C: Considering developmental levels for positive classroom environments, teachers can observe children's levels/types of play (unoccupied, independent, onlooker, parallel, associative, cooperative) and offer them not only matching activities (a), but also experiences at the next higher levels/types. Teachers must remember that older elementary and middle school students have not developed the social interaction skills of high school students, and accordingly guide them in peer collaboration (b). They should not expect new preschoolers to share, but instead should model, encourage, and reward sharing (c). For high school students, teachers can extend learning environments beyond classrooms (d) to surrounding communities, including service projects.

71. C: One of the descriptors for ELL students at the Intermediate level of Speaking proficiency is speaking in simple sentences, using mostly present tenses. Another is that they may often need to hesitate for long times (a) to figure out how to express themselves. Another descriptor is that they seldom have sufficient vocabulary to speak in more detail (b). People used to interacting with ELLs usually understand their pronunciation, but people unused to ELLs often will not (d).

72. A: When instruction is more demanding—e.g., when students are asked to solve novel problems and create products—teacher decisions are not simpler (c) but more complex. When teachers encourage student responsibility, both teachers and students approach and understand instructional content differently (b). Teachers must not only help students meet academic demands for comprehension and manipulation of subject content, but also help them meet social demands (d) for effective demonstration of their content knowledge in interactions with others.

73. C: Factors that can often prevent diverse parents and families from communicating and participating in the education of their children include language barriers, which frequently stop them from communicating (a); unsuccessful parent school histories, which can make them feel ineffectual to participate (b); feeling alienated from school processes because of their differing cultures (c) and/or languages; and poor past experiences with schools, which can make them reluctant to participate (d).

74. B: While parental involvement does not guarantee academic success, students whose parents are involved in their schooling typically perform better than students whose families are less involved. While many factors contribute to this outcome, one important factor is that by being involved, parents convey to their children their belief that education is valuable.

75. B: Ms. Kincaid should call the parents who have not responded to notify them directly about the conferences. When one strategy (sending notes) does not appear to be effective, the teacher should shift her strategy accordingly. Answer D is inappropriate because it is unfair to place the responsibility of getting parents to attend conferences on fourth grade students. Asking students directly (A) would also be inappropriate because it would not necessarily yield reliable information and it could also make students feel uncomfortable or "singled-out" on the basis of their parents' behavior.

76. A: The most important skills that students develop through problem solving activities are inquiry and critical thinking skills. While time management and social skills may be secondary benefits of such activities if they are conducted in groups, the ability to think critically is the primary benefit.

77. C: Behaviorist learning theory states that receiving rewards for certain behaviors reinforces the behavior, i.e., increases the probability the behavior will recur for more rewards. A student receiving positive reinforcement for studying hard will continue to do so. Social learning theory states people respond not only to direct rewards, but also to observing others receiving rewards, and will imitate rewarded behaviors. A student studying hard who observes struggling classmates getting more teacher attention may stop studying for comparable attention (a). A student observing classmates getting rewards for studying hard imitates the studying behavior (b). A student observing struggling classmates getting less attention continues studying hard (d) to avoid losing the rewards. Choice (c) is an example of behaviorist learning theory, the others of social learning theory.

78. C: By dividing her students into ability groups and spending at least one hour each week working with each group in a way that meets the members' unique needs (A), Ms. Morse is targeting various ability levels, but she is not necessarily targeting different learning styles or teaching the same lesson to the various groups. Differentiated instruction involves presenting a single lesson in a variety of ways that allow students of varying ability levels and learning styles to comprehend it.

79. C: Ringing a bell is the strongest signal for getting attention from the students. Just saying something might not be heard or might be ignored because the teacher is often talking, and a hand signal might not be seen. However, a bell makes a sound different from the usual human voice and is usually louder, too, so it makes the strongest attention-getting signal. Good teachers establish certain signals with their students as a form of shortcut communication. The most common is the signal for attention. Simply saying "Good morning" or "Let's get started" are good oral signals that the teacher wants all eyes on him/her so that a change of activity can begin. Hand signals such as just holding up a hand as a signal for quiet also work well.

80. C: While bullying among boys is usually displayed by obvious teasing and even violence, girls tend to use bullying tactics that are more discreet. For example, girls might spread false rumors about each other or exclude certain individuals from social activities. While parents and teachers are less likely to notice this type of bullying, it can be just a damaging to the victim's self esteem as violence.

81. D: If Mr. Gupta knows that it the experiments are where the time is being lost, then he needs to closely evaluate why they are taking so long. Are the students spending more time talking that working? Are they getting stuck and waiting a long time for Mr. Gupta to get around to them? Are some of the experiments simply too ambitious for this class? In any case, he must determine where the problem is, and then reorganize the way experiments are conducted to make the process more efficient. Answer A is too drastic, and deprives students of an important opportunity to gain a hands-on understanding of the principles being covered. Answer B is also not the way to go. This will eventually result in a class that fails to cover a lot of important material. Answer C is unfair to the students. Mr. Gupta should not overburden the students because he failed to properly organize the class in the first place.

82. B: Simply memorizing words from the Constitution or the Declaration of Independence does nothing to ensure that students actually understand the meaning behind the words. *Processing* means the activity requires students to interpret new material and to express it in an original way. Answer A requires the students to consider the Revolution from a modern perspective. Answer C requires the students to spend some time every day thinking about what they learned, which helps keep the new material active in their brains. Answer D requires the students to do their own research and ask and answer their own questions about important figures in the history of our country.

83. C: Scoring guides typically are published by the authors of the tests they accompany, not different authors (a); this is an advantage in minimizing inaccurate or inappropriate scoring or incorrect score interpretation, as the authors direct teachers/other scorers to follow procedures they designed for their tests. They do not force teachers to give specific scores to specific student responses (b); rather, they allow teachers reasonable flexibility to use their own best judgment with individual student responses and/or test conditions (d), an advantage. The possibility that scoring guides can be misinterpreted or misapplied by inexperienced users or those with poor judgment (c) is a disadvantage.

84. A: An advantage of intrinsic student motivation is that it has greater longevity than extrinsic student motivation via external rewards; it is also self-sustaining, unlike extrinsic motivation. The length of time it takes (b) for teacher preparation to develop it; the amount of individual differentiation it needs (c) for teachers to give different students; and the length of time it takes to work (d) for changing student behavior are all disadvantages.

85. A: Elements of critical thinking include distinguishing fact from opinion (c) in text or speech by looking for objectivity, facts, and proof vs. subjectivity, non-factual information, and absence of proof; finding evidence or no evidence (d) to support the writer or speaker's arguments by examining the text or speech; evaluating evidence used to support (a) arguments or statements by considering whether its source is reputable, proven, and accepted by authorities in the field; and judging the quality of material (b) or information by comparing it to other material/information, consulting one's own previous experience, and listening to one's own intuition.

86. B: Rewards and punishments given by teachers foster extrinsic motivation rather than intrinsic motivation. Components of intrinsic student motivation to learn include fascination with the subject matter (a); relevance of learning to real life (c); and recognition that learning enhances one's cognitive skills (d).

87. B: Conducting a teleconference with the parent while they're on their lunch break would probably not be effective because it would require students to gather around one speakerphone or each have their own phones. A videoconference could be arranged so all of the students can easily see the parent and the parent can see the students and respond to their questions, and Powerpoint or videotaping would also be effective at conveying the information if videoconferencing technology was not available.

88. D: Research studies have identified that teachers ask students they expect less from less challenging questions (a) than they ask others; call on them less often (b) than on others; explore their answers in less depth (c) than others' answers; and reward less rigorous responses from them (d) than the responses they reward from other students.

89. C: There should be follow-up to the conflict resolution to make certain that the children are sticking to their agreed-upon solution and to ensure that the conflict does not re-occur. Some teachers might feel that dropping the issue will help everyone forget the conflict, but that usually is not the case. Conflicts are best handled with calmness and a quiet voice as the teacher gathers information about the conflict in order to get a complete and fair picture of the situation. Then the teacher should review the conflict with the children and ask for their ideas for ways the problem could have been prevented and ways to solve the conflict. Involving the children in the resolution of the problem teaches them self-regulation and respect for themselves and others.

90. B: Assigning students to write about conflicts they have been involved in gives them time-out periods wherein they can cool off and reflect about events and their roles in them. Writing does not force students to ruminate over conflicts or extend them further (a); it enables them to analyze what happened, review their feelings, retrospectively consider alternatives (c) they might have chosen instead, and use the conflicts as learning opportunities (d).

91. D: Because of diverse student needs, teachers are required to ensure educational equity by differentiating their instruction accordingly with student abilities (a), offering equal opportunities to all students (b), treating all students fairly (c), and choosing and/or adapting instructional materials to reflect multicultural perspectives (d) to which multicultural students can relate.

92. B: Since most of the students in Ms. Frank's class are auditory learners, she would reach the majority of her students by teaching them a song about the new concept that they're learning. Auditory learners remember and comprehend concepts best using their sense of hearing.

93. C: Cognitive dissonance is a term coined by psychologist Leon Festinger to describe the discomfort we feel when considering contradictory information. We resolve this discomfort by rejecting certain information, or forming new schemata or changing existing ones to accommodate some information. This term is not related to a disorder (a), sensory overload (b), or incompatible instructional and learning (d) processes.

94. C: Embarrassing students in front of classmates and/or punishing them do NOT prevent, but actually incite, individual and group student rebellion. Showing interest in student work and encouraging students (a), alerting students to change their behaviors through physical proximity and touch (b), reminding students of times when they succeeded and modifying lesson presentations (d) to be more interesting than any distractors are all low-impact teacher interventions that prevent undesirable student behaviors from escalating.

95. A: Whereas behaviorist learning theorists believe that learning always results in some change in behavior, Bandura disagrees, finding children could learn something new without necessarily producing new/different behaviors. Bandura agrees with the behaviorist concept that consequences (events immediately following behaviors) either reward them, reinforcing/increasing their probable recurrence, or punish them, decreasing their probable recurrence. Unlike behaviorists who insist only externally observable, measurable behaviors can be changed, Bandura emphasizes the importance of internal cognitive processes in learning and thus of examining their roles (c); and of social interactions in learning (d).

96. C: Do not procrastinate about getting involved if a student is in danger of falling behind. Talk to the student kindly and find out what the problem is. It may not be what you expect. Answer A in quite simply not an effective way to keep tabs on your students. Moreover, it will likely create dissension among the class. Answer B does nothing to help a student who may be having trouble understanding the work. Answer D is only occasionally appropriate. Otherwise, the student will simply begin to assume that he can always get extra credit if he does not finish an assignment.

97. C: Copying the assigned homework questions from a textbook for a student who was home sick for a few days is unlikely to violate fair use standards for copyrighted material because it is a temporary, spontaneous use of a small portion of a copyrighted work. Generally, copying and using whole chapters or books (even e-books) is prohibited because it deprives the work's creators of income, and the same is true of copying and repeatedly using a DVD movie in class.

98. D: Circulating around the class allows the teacher to observe firsthand how things are going without interrupting the students' work. Answer A does not permit the teacher to see how the students are doing. Answer B is much too passive, and does not allow the teacher a chance to solve problems before they happen. Answer C is not practical, since it requires too much time.

99. C: Providing learning options is very useful in the middle grades because students are developing a sense of autonomy, and this allows them to exercise it. While the choices students make may reflect their self-concept or choice of peer group in some way, this is not the main area of development that such an exercise fosters. This exercise also reflects the fact that students have different learning styles, but this is not a developmental characteristic unique to middle school students.

100. A: In scaffolded instruction, first the teacher models performance of a new and/or difficult task and asks students to do Think-Alouds about it. The second step involves collaboration by students and teacher. The third step entails paired or small-group student work on the task, with teacher support as needed. In the fourth step, students practice the task independently.

101. A: The students always need to see the teacher as well as whatever is pertinent to the lesson around the room. No matter the activity or room arrangement, the teacher always needs to be able to get close to each student so that the teacher can give assistance wherever necessary. Small group work, individual work, or discussions may need furniture rearrangement to best facilitate the activity, so it is standard practice to move desks and tables around to suit the lesson. When students work in pairs or teams, it is important that the teacher selects the pairs or teams to ensure compatibility and good work while avoiding problems that might result from conflicts between students or good friends sitting next to each other and being more interested in personal matters than the lesson.

102. A: A free, appropriate public education (in the least restrictive environment possible) is a federal right guaranteed to students with qualifying disabilities under the IDEA. Reporting dangerous behaviors (b) to school staff is a student responsibility that varies by state or school district. Student rights to advocate for changes in policy (c) or law and to peaceful dispute resolution (d) also vary by state or district.

103. C: Once you know the necessary formula, a spreadsheet is the best tool to use for applying it across the board. While answer A will certainly work, and some people still prefer it, using a spreadsheet is much more efficient and will also guard against careless arithmetic errors. If you are unfamiliar with spreadsheets, it is well worth taking the time to learn, as it will greatly improve your efficiency in calculating grades.

104. C: The most effective way to evaluate the effectiveness of the new textbook would be to compare current students' improvement on a criterion-referenced test over the course of a year to previous students' improvement on that same test. This method would help to eliminate intervening variables (standardized test difficulty and changing focus, as well as variations in students' initial level of academic achievement) that would make the other measures suggested problematic.

105. B: Mr. Ainsley should respond to the principal's suggestion by using available professional development resources on assessment to develop a plan to improve his use of assessment in the classroom and present it to the principal for review. This approach will provide the most immediate and effective way to resolve the flaw in his instructional approach, and it will also allow him to get feedback from the principal so that he knows that he has correctly understood and responded to the principal's suggestion.

106. D: A Resident Teacher is one who is not a student teacher, not yet a teacher of record but being paid, and completing a practicum or residency supervised by a Master Teacher (c). A Novice Teacher (a) has certification but is still developing with a Master Teacher's partnership, and does not have but is eligible for tenure. A Teacher Leader (b), the highest level, works partly with administrators/leadership teams and partly in classrooms. A Master Teacher (c) is a key leadership team member, leading school teams and also sometimes working in both classrooms and faculty support.

107. A: Legal blindness is defined as 20/200, i.e., reading at 20' on a Snellen eye chart what one should be able to read at 200'. Seeing at from 20/200 to 20/70 (b) after correction in the better eye is labeled as low vision. Seeing at from 5/200 to 10/200 (c) is the definition of travel vision. Seeing at from 3/200 to 5/200 (d), which typically involves seeing moving objects, is called motion perception. Seeing at lower than 3/200, and seeing bright light at 3' but not movement, is called light perception.

108. B: At this level, it can often be difficult to sustain a productive discussion for longer than 15 minutes or so. After that, students will tend lose interest, or veer the discussion off topic.

109. C: Teachers should ask more than half of their questions at higher cognitive levels (i.e., requiring students to apply, analyze, evaluate, and synthesize or create information) for students in secondary grades, and include smaller proportions at this level for students in elementary grades, rather than by dividing question types equally for all grades (a), giving more high-level questions to all grades (b), or giving more low-level questions (i.e., requiring students only to remember and understand information) to all grades (d).

110. A: Words like "because" and "for example" have to be followed by a reasonably precise explanation that gives clarity to the communication. Clarity is critical to good communication. Vague or confusing language can reduce the effectiveness of presentations. Answer B gives examples of negated intensifiers; that is, the use of words such as "many" and "very" that indicate something big, but that are qualified by a "not", which communicates a nebulous state. Answer C indicates an ambiguous designation or destination – how is the student supposed to figure out needed specific information, even how to find supplies in the closet, if the directions are so vague? Answer D has words with the problem of vague probability; the student doesn't know exactly how often or what percentage.

111. C: Some students perform better on tests, while others do better with papers or other projects. Just as students learn in a variety of ways, their talents for expressing what they have learned also varies widely. A teacher that evaluates students based on a wide variety of tasks will come away with a much more complete picture of each student's strengths and weaknesses.

112. D: By FERPA regulations, schools may disclose student "directory" information without prior consent (a). This includes names, addresses, birth dates, birthplaces, attendance dates, honors and awards, phone numbers (b), etc. FERPA requires schools to notify parents and eligible students of their FERPA rights annually, but does permit disclosure (c) of this student "directory" information—provided they give parents/eligible students enough prior notice so they can request non-disclosure (d) if they choose.

113. C: Inductive reasoning is bottom-up and specific to general. It begins with accumulating specific observations, clues, or information; then identifies patterns or commonalities among these; and finally, based on the preponderance of evidence, draws conclusions about a general principle/theory. Deductive reasoning is top-down and general to specific (a). It begins with a general principle/theory/field of information; then, through deducting elements, narrows down to more a specific hypothesis; tests it through observations/data confirming or refuting it; and finally, based on the most specific evidence, draws conclusions about a specific effect/relationship. Choices (b) and (d) pair contradictory concepts.

114. C: The offended family will be given the opportunity to educate the teacher and the class about their culture. The activity should continue so that the other students aren't denied an opportunity to share because of the teacher's mistake. Most definitely, the teacher should not compound the error by persisting in asking for something that s/he has been told is offensive. Teachers who make assumptions based on cultural stereotypes could offend students with inappropriate statements or requests. It is good practice to have the students share about their cultures in a "Show and Tell" activity, for example. However, should the teacher make a mistake about cultural practices, s/he should apologize to anyone offended and not let the matter drop but follow up with another option and continue the activity for everyone. The teacher should give careful thought to the mistake and correct any misconceptions.

115. A: To communicate high expectations to all students, teachers should identify students they expect less from as soon as possible, because it is hard to accept or modify negative expectations already formed. Research finds student similarities influence teacher expectations, though teachers resist admitting this; therefore, experts advise teachers to identify similarities (b) for actively preventing biases from controlling their thoughts and/or behaviors. Since teacher behaviors have more influence than teacher expectations, not vice versa (c), teachers must identify their different behaviors toward low-expectancy students. They must also consciously treat high- and low-expectancy students the same, not differently (d).

116. B: students who are learning English as a second language typically have normal or above-average intelligence, although their academic performance may suffer because most assignments directly or indirectly require English language skills. Because English Language Learners are typically of normal intelligence, and because being an English Language Learner is not considered a disability, these students cannot be referred for special education services unless they have a true learning disability (A). Further, cultural background has no bearing on intelligence, so D is incorrect.

117. D: According to Piaget's theory, the distinction between people at the concrete operational stage (approximately 7-12 years of age) and the formal operational stage (approximately 12-16 years of age) of development is that Those in the concrete operational stage can think logically only with respect to concrete experiences, while those at the formal operational stage can reason in abstract and hypothetical terms. Children at the sensorimotor stage (birth to 2 years old) rely on their sensory perception and motor skills to learn and understand the world around them, and children at the preoperational stage (3-7) think in a literal, symbolic manner.

118. D: Studies show that computers are especially effective at getting students to exercise the kind of high-level logic and complex problem solving skills that they need to develop for use in professional situations.

119. C: Ms. Holloway should first contact the student's social services caseworker about the problem so that he or she can inform each of the students' successive foster parents of the importance of helping the student with math. While contacting the parents (B) would normally be the first step if the student were at home or with a permanent foster family, contacting the student's caseworker is more effective in a situation where a student is frequently shifted between different families. The caseworker can ensure that each successive family is aware of the student's academic status, and perhaps arrange ongoing math tutoring for him.

120. C: Task cards are a strategy best used as a manipulative for tactile-kinesthetic learners. While a task card may have writing on it, the value to tactile learners is that a card is something that the students can touch, which makes the writing more real to them. Students who are dominantly verbal-linguistic learners will learn best when listening, speaking, reading, and writing. Consequently, activities such as classroom discussions, listening to a story read by the teacher, or reading the words listed on the classroom word wall are good strategies for reaching the verbal-linguistic learners in the class.

121. A: When a student keeps his own grade book, it causes him to be more involved in his grade and to understand exactly where it is coming from. This way, he will know exactly how he is doing on any given day. Answer B is inappropriate. Reading students' grades to the class violates their right to privacy. Answer C is not a bad idea for some classes, but it does not necessarily keep the student informed of his/her own progress. Answer D is a good idea, but it also would generate a lot of extra work for the teacher, and does not involve the student as directly.

122. A: FERPA provides that schools may furnish student records without prior consent to some researchers if they are conducting certain studies on behalf of the school; by court order or legal subpoena (b); to appropriate personnel in safety or health emergencies (c); and to juvenile justice system authorities, according to specific state laws (d).

123. B: The definition of independent study encompasses not only the individual student working alone (a), but also two students working as partners (c) or small groups of students (d) working together. In fact, teachers can even use independent study as an instructional strategy with the whole class. Regardless of the number of students, independent study is less teacher-centered/teacher-directed; the teacher functions as a facilitator and guide. Provided they have developed the required skills, students have more autonomy and choices with independent study.

124. A: Evaluating individual student progress will make evaluation much fairer in such a situation. Answer B is more about making the teacher look good than about fairness to the students. Answer C, shifting the grading priority to research projects, will not necessarily make the evaluations fairer if student progress is not considered. Answer D is the opposite of what a teacher should do in this situation.

125. C: Although students work more independently in research projects and other forms of independent instruction than in more teacher-directed activities, teachers still provide students with guidance, but only as needed. Teachers do not assign research questions (a); students develop these independently. Students, not teachers, also locate and access information sources (b) for research. Students write reports or papers to communicate their research results, with teacher guidance (d) if they need it.

126. A: One advantage of writing anecdotal notes as an assessment tool is that teachers can collect information about student skills and behaviors outside of assessment activities as well as during them; this can help teachers realize valuable insights into student learning and behavior. The fact that such notes are not standardized unless the teacher incorporates norms or criteria for comparison (b) is a disadvantage. An advantage of anecdotal notes is that teachers *can* record observations of individual student behaviors, which standard test instruments, checklists, and most other tools do *not* allow (c). The fact that anecdotal notes often lack any supporting context (d) is a disadvantage.

127. D: To create supportive classroom climates, teachers should arrange the furniture and materials to promote student comfort (a), dialogue (b), ownership (c), and collaboration (d).

128. B: The most effective strategy for Mr. Swanson to use would be to explain to the students that they have done a good job of improving their behavior, but that they can do even better. As a consequence, they now need to earn four check marks to get the reward, which is 45 minutes on the computer. This strategy has several advantages over the other options presented here. Unlike A and D, this strategy maintains consistency with the previous plan, and it also increases the reward in proportion to the expected improvement in behavior. C would not be effective because it increases the reward without requiring a commensurate improvement in behavior.

129. C: *Constructive assertiveness* means that a teacher is confidently in control of the class and communicates clearly without losing control of his/her emotions. Such a teacher also easily adapts to different situations and different points of view. Answer A is an example of a teacher who is extremely inflexible. This is not constructive assertiveness. Answer B is an example of a teacher who is unable to control the class. Answer D illustrates a teacher who fails to control his/her emotions. This is a sign of weakness and insecurity.

130. B: The answer uses a negative and is just like saying, "Eat your spinach because it is good for you." Kids want to do what they like, not necessarily what's good for them. Answer A is a positive communication that creates anticipation for learning because the teacher is setting expectations and giving students a goal for achieving a skill that might be interesting. Answer C sets up an expectation of curiosity that encourages students to want to find out more. Answer D is another way that a teacher can interest students who have a curiosity about the teacher's personal life, and is very inviting because it offers to share something with the students.

Practice Test #2

1. Which of the following is the best example of a learning experience that would prompt students to explore educational content from varied and integrated perspectives?

    a. Taking a computer-administered test
    b. Reading about life in a different country
    c. Using flashcards to study for a vocabulary test
    d. Writing a research report about an animal of the students' choice

2. Getting the classroom ready for the first day of school can be overwhelming for a new teacher. As the big day comes, one often must make some hard choices and leave a few things to be done later. Which of the following could wait a few more days if necessary?

    a. Optimize arrangement of student desks
    b. Decorate all bulletin boards and set them up for display
    c. Make sure that you have enough textbooks and that they are all in satisfactory condition
    d. Verify that equipment such as overhead projectors and computer workstations are functional and ready to use

3. Which of the following is least likely to cause a sudden academic decline:

    a. Parental divorce
    b. Drug abuse
    c. Eating disorders
    d. Participation in a school sports team

4. How does the theory of multiple intelligences address the learning needs of students?

    a. It suggests quite simply that some students are smarter than others, and that teachers must accept that while a *C* is a bad grade for some students, that it is a very good grade for others.
    b. It suggests that different people learn in different ways, and that teachers can give more students a better chance by using a variety of teaching methods in the classroom.
    c. It suggests that every student has only two areas of talent in which he or she can excel, and that once these talents are identified, students should not be pushed in other areas.
    d. It suggests that all students are equally intelligent and that they will learn if they are motivated enough.

5. Your 9th grade biology class is about to take on its first animal dissection. You have already covered the procedure in detail during class, but you know that some of the students are still feeling nervous or even a little queasy. What else can you do to help make the dissection go more smoothly?

    a. Remind them that medical students regularly dissect human cadavers, and that this is not really such a big deal
    b. Set a timer for each section of the procedure, so the students stay on pace
    c. Require each student write out their own step-by-step explanation of what they plan to do
    d. Have the students speak out loud as they work, describing what they are doing

6. In regard to the process of writing a lesson plan, which of the following is true?

a. The steps of writing the plan may vary with the teaching model.
b. Experienced teachers won't need to write down as much as new teachers because some actions become automatic with time.
c. The lesson's opening, body, and closing should be written in order.
d. Only the parts of the lesson to be presented to the students need to be written down, not necessarily the pre-planning and editing tasks.

7. Which of the following is a characteristic of K-12 ELL students at the Beginning proficiency level in Listening.

a. Easily understanding simple conversation on familiar topics
b. Easily understanding simple discussion with cues/supports
c. Observing others for cues, but not requesting clarifications
d. Requesting clarifications, but not observing others for cues

8. Mr. Bennet's fourth-grade students are practicing digital literacy skills as part of a math unit on financial literacy. They will be completing two digital assignments during this unit. One assignment is to write a blog post on budgeting that will be published on the school website. Another assignment is to write an email to a friend describing something they are saving up to buy. Which topic would be most beneficial for Mr. Bennet to teach to assist students with successfully completing both of these assignments?

a. Verifying online sources
b. Selecting relevant search keywords
c. Navigating nonlinear writing and hyperlinks in digital texts
d. Adjusting formality of language based on audience

9. Mike, a student in your 10th grade geometry class, is rapidly falling behind in class because he is having a harder time grasping concepts than are most of the other students. You have set up a meeting with Mike's parents and want to discuss options such as encouraging them to hire a private tutor, or possibly even transferring him to a remedial math class. What might be the best way to begin the discussion?

a. "Mike is working very hard in my class, but he is having a very tough time. I wanted to discuss a few ideas with you, and also to hear your input about what we can do to help him."
b. "Mike currently has one of the lowest averages in my class. I want to be frank with you. If something does not change, I'm afraid he will fail the class."
c. "Have you been working much with Mike at home to help him with his geometry? He just does not seem to be cutting it."
d. "Mike is having a little trouble with his geometry. I'm sure he will do fine, but I just wanted to let you know."

10. A student is able to apply strategies to comprehend the meanings of unfamiliar words; can supply definitions for words with several meanings such as *crucial*, *criticism*, and *witness*; and is able to reflect on her background knowledge in order to decipher a word's meaning. These features of effective reading belong to which category?

a. Word recognition
b. Vocabulary
c. Content
d. Comprehension

11. Which of the following statements best describes the type of education that the Individuals with Disabilities Education Act of 2004 (IDEA) requires for all students with identified emotional and learning disabilities?

    a. A free and appropriate education, even in cases where the student has been suspended or expelled from school
    b. An appropriate education, except in cases where the student's behavior causes him or her to be expelled from school
    c. A free education that is conducted outside of the general education classroom
    d. An appropriate education that must be paid for by the student's family

12. Which of the following is *not* a good example of the type of verb one should use to express the desired behavior component in an objective?

    a. Calculate
    b. Know
    c. Define
    d. Predict

13. Mrs. Fillmore is teaching her fourth grade class about fractions, and she wants to explain to the students why multiplying two fractions together yields a smaller fraction. Which of the following methods would most effectively communicate this concept?

    a. Giving the students a list of proper fractions, and asking them to multiply any two of the fractions together in order to demonstrate that a smaller fraction is always the product.
    b. Explaining that multiplying two fractions together produces a fraction of a fraction, and using manipulatives to demonstrate this.
    c. Verbally explaining to the students that multiplying a fraction by a whole number produces a larger number, and multiplying a fraction by a fraction produces a smaller fraction.
    d. Demonstrating that when you divide the product of two fractions by one of the fractions, the result is the other fraction.

14. Which of the following activities would best help to create a classroom environment that promotes a love of reading for kindergarten students?

    a. Going on a word hunt to locate words starting with a specific letter
    b. Tracing sight words using stencils
    c. Practicing phonics skills on the classroom computer
    d. Reading a favorite rhyming text aloud together and discussing favorite parts

15. Legal and ethical requirements of classroom teachers include which of these?

    a. Teachers are required to keep student records confidential, but not other information.
    b. Teachers are required to protect the privacy of any or all student personal information.
    c. Teachers are required to seek, but not get permission, to utilize copyrighted materials.
    d. Teachers are required to ask only authors for permission to use copyrighted materials.

16. An English Language Development (ELD) teacher notices that one of his English learners is refusing to use his home language in school. He has started to hang out with native English speakers and dressing similarly to them. What is this phenomenon known as?

    a. Accommodation
    b. Biculturalism
    c. Culture Shock
    d. Assimilation

17. Which method of lesson planning will help a teacher ensure that his/her lesson will take advantage of the multiple intelligences of different students?

    a. Use a lesson-planning matrix to help devise learning activities that are organized according to different abilities

    b. Survey the students about what helps them to learn the most

    c. Design a seating plan so that the students who need the most help sit in the front

    d. Try to use more images and graphs in presentations

18. What is the most accurate predictor of a student's achievement in school?

    a. Socio-economic background of a student's peers

    b. Family involvement in student's life

    c. Education level of parents

    d. Marital status of parents

19. A student has exposed himself to a female student in the back of the classroom. What is the only acceptable response by the teacher?

    a. Assign the offending student to detention

    b. Lock the offending student in a closet

    c. Send the offending student to the principal's office or call the police

    d. Paddle the offending student in front of the class

20. Mrs. Brown is becoming frustrated because her sixth grade students begin packing up their materials in anticipation of the bell while she is still teaching. Students most likely engage in this behavior because:

    a. Sixth grade students tend to have very short attention spans, and the students are bored with her teaching

    b. Students at this age don't want to stand out, so when one student starts packing up her materials, all of the other students are likely to follow

    c. Sixth grade students have difficulty sitting still, and they are anxious to get up and move around

    d. Middle school students, especially sixth-graders, tend to be anxious about completing transitions

21. Which of the following is an ethical or legal violation?

    a. Physically restraining a student who is acting violently or endangering others

    b. Informing a student's parents of the student's current grades

    c. Approaching a student and asking if the student has a learning disability

    d. Refusing to excuse a student during class to go to the bathroom

22. Which of the following is *not* a benefit of flexible grouping practices?

    a. Allows students to work at individual interest levels.

    b. Allows students to pick their own groups for better cooperation.

    c. Allows students to work according to readiness levels.

    d. Allows students to work on specific skills identified as deficient through assessments.

23. Which learning theory is based on the idea that students are actively involved in constructing their own meaning, and that teachers should guide students through scaffolding rather than using instructor-led teaching techniques?

 a. Behaviorism
 b. Cognitivism
 c. Constructivism
 d. Social learning theory

24. Which equipment should be arranged first when deciding upon a classroom floor plan?

 a. The teacher's desk
 b. Computer workstations
 c. Filing cabinets
 d. Overhead projector

25. Which of the following statements best explains why middle school students' academic performance can be most effectively assessed by focusing on progress, rather than comparisons with other students?

 a. Focusing on progress makes it possible for all students to earn good grades, even if they are struggling academically
 b. Since middle school students are so developmentally diverse, focusing on progress allows teachers to maintain high expectations while meeting students where they are academically
 c. By focusing on progress, it is easier for teachers to justify the fact that many of their students are not meeting grade level expectations
 d. By the middle school level, some students have fallen irreversibly behind, and using a progress-focused assessment approach prevents students from being retained

26. Models of behavior modification typically use which of the following to effect changes?

 a. What the individual is thinking
 b. What the individual is sensing
 c. What the individual is feeling
 d. What the individual is doing

27. Mr. Gonzalez has noticed that one of his students, Benji, has experienced a rapid decline in his academic performance over the past few weeks. Benji seems unusually sluggish on some days and abnormally restless on other days. He frequently arrives late to school, saying that he overslept. Which of the following is the most likely explanation for this change in Benji's behavior?

 a. Benji has developed a learning disability, and should be screened for special education services
 b. Benji's unpredictable behavior is normal for an adolescent and should not be cause for concern
 c. Benji's behavior signals that he might be using illegal drugs
 d. Benji is probably experiencing depression, and should be referred to the school counselor

28. What is the best method for improving students' memorization skills?

 a. Repetition
 b. Break the item to be memorized into small sections and then learn the sections one at a time
 c. Students should read the item once as rapidly as possible, and then immediately try to repeat as much as they can recall
 d. Play a distinctive piece of music in the background

29. Which example best demonstrates a student making an accommodation to existing schema, as suggested by Piaget?

a. A child knows that periods are used at the ends of sentences. When given a question to punctuate for the first time, she uses a period.
b. After using the writing process to write a narrative text, a child applies the process to write an expository text.
c. A child does not like bees until learning about the role they play in pollination. She then believes that bees are helpful.
d. A toddler learns about lions from a picture book and practices saying, "Roar!" She hears a tiger making a similar sound at the zoo and calls it a lion.

30. Ms. Schneider, a fifth grade teacher, has been assigned a paraprofessional who comes to her class three times a week to work with the mainstreamed special education students. For the past week, the paraprofessional has arrived late to the classroom and appeared distracted and disinterested in his duties. What should be the first step that Ms. Schneider takes to resolve the problem?

a. Ask the school principal to assign a different paraprofessional to her class
b. Send a note to the special education teacher explaining the problem
c. Take the paraprofessional aside and explain her concerns
d. Help the special education students write a letter to the paraprofessional explaining how his behavior is affecting their learning

31. How can adults support adolescent development in the affective, social, and moral domains?

a. Help teens to plan ahead for situations involving peer pressure and/or risky behaviors.
b. Respect teen needs for privacy by not showing interest in/asking about their activities.
c. Avoid asking about suicidal ideations, which can escalate depression common in teens.
d. Attribute all behavior changes observed to adolescence and do not investigate further.

32. Suppose a particularly promising student in your 11th grade physics class has become increasingly arrogant to the point that it is disrupting with your lessons. The student constantly complains out loud in class that the problems are too easy, and often blurts the answer to a problem out before you have even finished explaining it. The student is, in fact, one of your best students, and the class is probably not advanced enough for him. However, he must complete this class before moving on to more advanced science classes. How might a teacher best go about resolving the problem?

a. Discipline the student by lowering his grades
b. Try to come up with two or three options that could resolve the problem and work with the student to commit to one of them
c. Recommend to the student's parents that they might want to consider enrolling him in a physics class at the local community college
d. Send the student to the vice principal's office

49

33. Mr. Holt is a new teacher, and has been teaching for three months. He is painfully aware that he is having trouble controlling his class. He knows that it is not simply a matter of one or two students being "bad apples." He is unable to effectively control his students and he feels intimidated. What should he do?

a. Be patient and give it a few more months. It takes time for a new teacher to find his stride and establish himself.
b. He must get control of the class immediately. Dole out harsh punishments to the whole class every time someone misbehaves. The students will be back in line in no time.
c. Inform the principal that he is a new teacher and request that the principal let him swap classes with another teacher who has students that are easier to get along with.
d. Consult with other teachers and administrators at your school and ask for advice and assistance.

34. Which example best demonstrates a student learning in his zone of proximal development?

a. Being taught to apply a decoding strategy while reading a book at the instructional level
b. Practicing fluency using a familiar reading passage
c. Listening to an audio version of a story that is too difficult to read independently
d. Pairing up with a struggling reader to model use of a comprehension strategy

35. The educator's code of ethics does not prohibit which of the following activities?

a. Interfering with the political rights of a colleague
b. Misrepresenting official district policies
c. Accepting gifts openly offered in appreciation of service
d. Revealing confidential student information without a lawful professional purpose or legal requirement

36. What is the best time to establish direct contact with a student's parents?

a. On the first day of school
b. Whenever a student makes a mistake
c. As soon as you notice a negative pattern developing in the student's work or behavior
d. Only when a problem becomes extreme

37. After reading a historical fiction short story, a teacher gives a struggling reader a graphic organizer containing the following sentence stems: *Someone, Wanted, But, So, Then.* This graphic organizer would best help the student with which skill?

a. Inferring
b. Summarizing
c. Drawing conclusions
d. Evaluating

38. What is the best tactic to use for displaying information in class if you must float from classroom to classroom?

a. Whatever classroom you are assigned to teach in is "yours" for that class period. Simply erase whatever is on the chalkboard and write your own information there.
b. Explain to the students that they need to take very thorough notes and give your lecture orally, without using any visual aides
c. Email your notes and diagrams to all the students in advance so that they can print them out at home and bring them to class
d. Prepare your notes on transparencies and display them using an overhead projector

39. All of the following statements are true about the evaluation component of a lesson except:

    a. Evaluation may be group-wide instead of individual.
    b. Evaluation must occur in some form with every lesson.
    c. Evaluation may occur on an on-going basis.
    d. Evaluation may occur again; for example, during a unit test.

40. In resolving behavior problems, a teacher should strive to be:

    a. Consistent and judgmental
    b. Consistent and objective
    c. Patient and collaborative
    d. Authoritative and judgmental

41. In designing the group project, Mr. Aaron wants to implement an assessment system that provides incentives for all students to contribute equally to the project and that is fair to students in cases where certain group members contribute more than others. Which of the following strategies would be most effective in helping him to achieve this objective?

    a. Giving all students in the group the opportunity to confidentially rate the contributions of their fellow group members, and giving lower grades to students who are rated lower by the members of their group
    b. Giving all students in the group the same grade so they'll be motivated to monitor one another's contributions and exercise teamwork skills
    c. Asking students to submit a report detailing exactly what their contribution was to the project, and to provide a self-evaluation of the value of their own contribution
    d. Grading the projects using a pass/fail system, since it is very difficult to equitably grade group projects

42. According to the Family Educational Rights and Privacy Act (FERPA), which of the following is true?

    a. Students of any age can refuse to disclose educational records to their parents
    b. Parents of children under 18 can inspect and request amendments to their children's educational records on demand
    c. Teachers need written authorization from parents in order to disclose a student's educational record a school official with a legitimate educational interest
    d. Written authorization from parents is required before a school releases a student's educational records to a school to which that student is transferring

43. Studies show that, when children start school with language deficits, the main cause is

    a. that these children predominantly come from specific socioeconomic groups.
    b. that these children lack supportive home, peer, and community environments.
    c. that these children predominantly come from particular cultural backgrounds.
    d. that these children mostly represent learners of English as a foreign language.

44. The alphabetic principle would be best introduced at which of Piaget's cognitive stages of development?

    a. Sensorimotor stage
    b. Preoperational stage
    c. Concrete operational stage
    d. Formal operational stage

45. When instructing ESL students with language learning disabilities, what should classroom teachers avoid?

    a. Using frequent modeling
    b. Slower rates of speaking
    c. Multisensory instruction
    d. Slang and idiomatic uses

46. Which is an example of the how technology can be used to take advantage of the theory of multiple intelligences?

    a. Students using the computer for math drills
    b. Teaching students to use a word processor for writing papers
    c. Offer students the option of doing class projects in the form of a blog or a video presentation
    d. Instead of a lecture, give lessons using PowerPoint presentations

47. Which of the following options is true of children in the pre-alphabetic stage of word learning?

    a. Children do not use any letter/sound relationships to decode words.
    b. Children use letter/sound relationships to correctly decode the initial or final sounds in words.
    c. Children use letter/sound relationships to correctly decode all sounds in simple, age-appropriate words.
    d. Children recognize and use letter groupings, along with letter/sound relationships, to decode words.

48. Which of the following is the best example of giving ESL students appropriate feedback in response to their developing English-language skills?

    a. Correcting every single mistake every time a student makes one
    b. Pointing out serious errors after the class has finished an activity
    c. Disregarding student errors in planning additional class practicing
    d. Accepting good work via silence while highlighting only mistakes

49. Objectives should be designed to teach something that is worth learning. Practicing skills is a good learning objective if the practice is embedded within application opportunities. Which of the following, however, may be a pointless practice?

    a. Reading to practice word attack skills.
    b. Solving problems to practice number facts and computations.
    c. Writing a composition to practice spelling and penmanship.
    d. Copying definitions of words to improve vocabulary.

50. When the middle schools receive the test results later on, they see that the students' scores are reported in both raw and scaled form. The scaled scores will be most useful for:

    a. Determining exactly how many questions students got right and wrong
    b. Determining which types of questions students had the most trouble with
    c. Comparing students' performance across different administrations of the same test
    d. Predicting students' performance in the classroom and on future tests

51. What was the result of cultural incompatibility theory being applied to schools?

    a. Schools were more understanding of different cultures.
    b. It perpetuated the status quo with the school, expecting home cultures to change.
    c. Schools fostered multicultural perspectives through incorporating diverse curricula.
    d. Schools demanded English-only programs.

52. Which of the following is a good example of appropriate content for an objective?

    a. Compare and contrast science fiction and fantasy.
    b. Complete Unit 6 in the vocabulary book.
    c. Describe the similarities and differences of setting between the stories "Wilderness Adventure" and "PS 139."
    d. Solve the arithmetic problems on p. 114 in your textbook.

53. What is the best way to ensure overall good behavior from your students?

    a. Establish a set of rules for your classroom, give the students a written copy, and go over the rules at the beginning of the year or semester
    b. A good teacher is a strict teacher. From the very beginning be gruff with the students, and show them that you have no tolerance for "nonsense."
    c. Wait a few days before setting ground rules. Students will respect you more if you give them more leeway in the beginning as they are settling in.
    d. Change your rules frequently to keep the students on their toes.

54. A fourth-grade teacher has a new English learner who has recently immigrated to the United States and enrolled in her class halfway through the school year. She notices that this student seems eager to participate and share about her culture. Which stage is this student experiencing in the acculturation process?

    a. Euphoria
    b. Cultural fatigue
    c. Adjustment
    d. Culture shock

55. Mr. Johnson is a sixth-grade language arts teacher. He wants to help his students assess their own growth in writing skills over the course of the year. Which type of assessment method would most likely help Mr. Johnson achieve his goal?

    a. Norm-referenced writing tests
    b. Criterion-referenced writing tests
    c. Performance-based tasks
    d. Writing portfolios

56. Which of the following activities would be most developmentally appropriate to include in a prekindergarten reading center?

    a. A consonant blend word sort
    b. Word cards that students can sequence to form sentences
    c. Letter outlines for students to fill in with beans
    d. Compound word puzzles

57. Providing opportunities for self-assessment is important primarily because:

    a. It increases students' feeling of control over their grades
    b. It helps to foster students' growing sense of autonomy
    c. It prepares students to evaluate their own work in the absence of an instructor
    d. It gives students a stake in the assessment process and fosters their sense of fairness

58. How can you best ensure that your students quickly settle down at the beginning of class so that you can get on with your lesson?

    a. Establish a firm routine for the beginning of every class, so that all the students know what to expect
    b. Use the time while the students are settling in to catch up on paper work
    c. Threaten to send the whole class to detention
    d. Tell the students that they can leave early if the class gets started on time

59. Which of the following strategies would foster students' intrinsic motivation to learn?

    a. Helping students to develop a personal connection to and interest in the material they're learning
    b. Emphasizing the rewards associated with academic success (recognition, a good job) and consequences associated with academic failure (shame, punishment by parents)
    c. Both A and B
    d. Neither A nor B

60. Which strategy is key for managing in-class group work sessions?

    a. Avoid spending too much time with any one group, even if that group is falling behind
    b. Make sure that none of the students in any group are good friends
    c. Avoid the temptation to walk around the room and interact with the groups
    d. Grade only the final result of the assignment, and not the students' individual participation

61. Of the following theories of cognitive development, whose posits discrete developmental stages?

    a. Skinner's
    b. Vygotsky's
    c. Bandura's
    d. Piaget's

62. Among theories of language acquisition, which idea is MOST compatible with the observation that children develop language in similar patterns across various cultural contexts?

    a. B. F. Skinner's environmental influence
    b. Whorf's linguistic relativity hypothesis
    c. Noam Chomsky's biological influences
    d. Neural networks theories of language

63. Which of the following assessment methods is most likely to be used in a learner-centered classroom?

    a. A method that provides different alternatives for students to demonstrate their knowledge
    b. A method that allows students to complete the assessment in groups
    c. A structured method that allows students' mastery to be compared with that of other students
    d. A multiple-choice test which students help to construct and grade

64. Mrs. Thomas recently taught her fifth grade students a new math concept that they seemed to understand clearly. However, when she administered a unit test of the material, more than half of the students failed. Mrs. Thomas' first reaction should be to:

  a. Give the students another chance to learn the material by re-teaching it the same way as she did the first time
  b. Analyze the test and the results to determine whether the assessment was well-designed and fairly administered
  c. Review the test results to discover exactly which aspect of the material the students had trouble with
  d. Compare her students' test results with the performance of last year's fifth grade class on the same test to see if there is a discrepancy

65. The best approach to using technology in the classroom is:

  a. Expect to teach technology with your subject.
  b. Rely on the school's technology center rather than your own classroom.
  c. Use only the technology with which you are comfortable.
  d. Increasing technology will improve instruction.

66. Mr. Fields wants to design an assessment method for his sixth grade math class that will help his students learn from their assignments and motivate them to improve. Which of the following approaches is most likely to accomplish this objective?

  a. Assigning ungraded homework problems and having weekly tests
  b. Assigning nightly homework problems that are peer-graded in class the next day, and going over the answers after the assignment is graded
  c. Assigning homework problems that are graded by the teacher and returned on the day before the unit test
  d. Assigning nightly homework problems which are graded and returned with a correct answer key within three days

67. Mr. Norton has noticed that some of the students within the teaching team that he is part of are in constant conflict with one another. He has tried disciplining the students according to school protocol, but the problem behavior has continued. Mr. Norton has called a meeting of the teachers on the team to discuss a strategy to deal with the problem. Which of the following steps should the teachers take first?

  a. Hold a diversity workshop for their students
  b. Take the students involved in the conflict aside and tell them that some of them will have to be moved to a different teaching team if they do not stop fighting
  c. Refer the students to the school's peer mediation program
  d. Hold a team meeting to renegotiate the team rules with the students' input

68. "Language load" refers to:

  a. The basic vocabulary words a first grader has committed to memory
  b. The number of unrecognizable words an English Language Learner encounters when reading a passage or listening to a teacher
  c. The damage that carrying a pile of heavy books could cause to a child's physique
  d. The number of different languages a person has mastered.

69. Which is the most effective tactic for getting through to resistant or hostile parents?

a. Establish yourself as an authority figure. Make it clear that parents are being negligent if they do not heed your recommendations and ensure that their children behave and complete their assignments.
b. Keep the meeting short. Tell the parents what the problem is and then tell them that you have another meeting in a few minutes.
c. Avoid placing blame and do your best to show that you genuinely care about their child
d. Be blunt. If you do not make sure that the parents understand the seriousness of the problem, they will become even more hostile when the problem gets worse.

70. Many of the students in your 9th grade algebra class seem bored, and even though they are smart, they are having trouble following your class. What actions could you take that might get the students more involved?

a. Devote one entire class period as a question-and-answer session. Encourage the students to ask you about any aspect of the subject which they are having difficulty learning
b. Set aside two class periods and meet with each student individually to address the problems they are having
c. Revisit topics you have already covered so that you can make sure that everyone understands
d. Periodically ask the students to meet in small groups and to come up with scenarios in which the kinds of problems you are covering can be applied

71. Which one of the following statements about objectives is *not* true?

a. Objectives are a communications tool aimed specifically at the students, not other audiences.
b. Objectives provide a way to evaluate student learning.
c. Objectives help focus and motivate students.
d. Objectives provide a way for teachers to measure their own effectiveness.

72. ELL students at the Advanced ELP level for Listening and Speaking are generally able to do which of the following?

a. They can speak grade-level English socially and academically without pauses.
b. They understand basic conversation/discussion with no need of clarification.
c. They can use abstract vocabulary and complex grammar without any errors.
d. They mispronounce words, but unfamiliar others usually understand them.

73. Which of the following is *not* a good example of a learning condition given in an objective?

a. On graph paper
b. During partner practice
c. After completing the unit on World War I
d. Given a list of European countries

Copyright © Mometrix Media. You have been licensed one copy of this document for personal use only. Any other reproduction or redistribution is strictly prohibited. All rights reserved.

74. Mr. Ferris has asked his eighth grade language arts students to submit their 500-word book reports in Microsoft Word format electronically via email. In terms of assessment, the main advantage of this method is that:

a. Mr. Ferris can grade the term papers more quickly and return them electronically so as not use up valuable class time while passing them out
b. Mr. Ferris can easily determine whether or not each student's report is the correct length
c. Mr. Ferris can use the change-tracking device in Microsoft Word to show the students how to improve their papers
d. Mr. Ferris can tabulate the number of specific grammatical errors the students have made in order to determine areas that he should focus on in class

75. Physically and cognitively, what do experts recommend adults do to support adolescent development?

a. Be vigilant for eating disorders and available to offer support and advice on college/career plans.
b. Provide adolescents with strict rules and direction rather than providing only support and advice.
c. Point out but not create opportunities to use problem solving, conflict resolution, and judgment.
d. Avoid advising teens to live healthful lifestyles, as they will resist this and would not do it anyway.

76. Shortly after the first day of class, you decide to send out a mass email to the parents of all of your students. What is the most important information that you can share in such an email?

a. A specific list of the requirements that students must meet in order to make good grades in your class.
b. A list of websites that parents can use as reference to help their children with the subject.
c. A detailed list of what you will be covering during each week of class.
d. A list of books that you expect all parents to read if they intend to be able to help their children.

77. Of the practices listed below, which would be most likely to promote a productive classroom environment for older elementary to middle-level students?

a. Providing opportunities for students to work cooperatively with peers
b. Frequently changing classroom routines to keep students engaged
c. Encouraging students to work independently to improve their ability to self-direct
d. Avoiding kinesthetic and active learning activities that overexcite students

78. Suppose you have gone back to teaching after taking a few years off to spend with your young children. During the first couple of weeks in your new job, you notice that your classroom setup seems a little outdated compared with those of some of the other teachers. What should you do?

a. It is your classroom, and you have a right to run it as you see fit.
b. Do your best to make your classroom mimic the other classrooms for your grade.
c. Speak to some of your fellow teachers and ask them where they got their ideas, and what they can tell you about the latest trends.
d. Ask the students how they think you should set up the room.

79. Mr. Stratton has assigned his fifth grade social studies class to write a research report about a historical period that they have learned about in class during the year. To ensure that students understand what is expected of them and are able to complete the project on schedule, the best approach for Mr. Stratton to take would be to:

a. Take time to explain how to do the research and set several 'checkpoints' before projects are due

b. Pair students who have never completed a research project before with students who have

c. Hold after-school tutoring sessions to help students brainstorm ideas and conduct research

d. Send a note home to parents telling them about the project and the due date

80. At one school, a large proportion of ESL students are very recent immigrants to America. To help these students and their families understand the protocols and culture of the school better before the school year starts, the ESL teachers will host an orientation event. What should the teachers do first to enable understanding and present helpful information most effectively during this event?

a. They should provide families with a detailed analysis of the district ESL program.

b. They should ask the ESL students to function as interpreters with their families.

c. They should provide families with pertinent materials in their native languages.

d. They should arrange discussion groups for all families on their native languages.

81. How does assigning term papers, or other long-term assignments, help students to learn skills about real life?

a. It gets them accustomed to being under a lot of stress

b. It does not; it only gives them an opportunity to cheat since they will not be working under teacher supervision

c. It teaches the importance of time-management and planning for unexpected circumstances

d. Such projects are rarely worth the effort, since more often than not, the parents end up doing most of the project

82. Which of the following is typically the most effective way to state classroom rules?

a. Rules should be stated negatively (do not speak out of turn)

b. Rules should be stated positively (students will treat one another with respect)

c. Rules should be phrased politely (please don't chew gum)

d. Rules should use detailed and specific language to describe what is prohibited (don't hit, slap, kick, pinch, or shove other students)

83. The school English Department is looking to reform its curriculum to become more multicultural. Which would be the best step to take to accomplish this?

a. Including books that feature diverse characters from around the world

b. Participating in professional development to incorporate technology in the curriculum

c. Brainstorming guest speakers who can come to talk about culture

d. Focusing on validating student's cultural identities through redesigning units

84. Whose responsibility is it to ensure that a teacher remains current with new teaching techniques?

a. The county school system is required to set the standards and provide opportunities for teachers to learn new skills.
b. The principal is responsible for ensuring that the teachers in his or her school do not fall behind.
c. The senior teachers for each grade are responsible for taking the less experienced teachers under their wing.
d. Every teacher is responsible to taking the initiative for learning and applying new teaching methods as appropriate for the classes they teach.

85. Which of the following is an example of how a math teacher might create lessons on fractions that take advantage of the theory of multiple intelligences?

a. Writing out fractions problems out on the chalkboard
b. Having students work in pairs to solve math problems
c. Explain how fractions are used practically in real life
d. Use music to illustrate how fractions work by letting students hear the difference between a whole note, a half note, and a quarter note

86. All of the options below are important, but which is the single most important element of creating a productive classroom environment?

a. A well decorated classroom
b. A clean classroom
c. Planning
d. A good seating arrangement

87. Mrs. Schubert is taking her biology class on a field trip to the local natural science museum. What can she do to ensure that her students make the most of the opportunity?

a. Tell the students to pay attention during the tour
b. Tell the students not to speak during the tour
c. Ask the students to take notes, and tell them that the notes will be graded
d. Give the students a pop quiz before going on the field trip

88. Mr. Krick recently read an article about a new interactive computer game that is very effective at getting children interested in history. Although he has never seen the game himself, he is interested in the possibility of using it with his class. What is the best course of action for Mr. Krick?

a. Go the local computer store, buy the game, and try it out with his class the next day
b. He should forget about it. Computer games are bad for children.
c. Make a copy of the article, note the website of the game, and consult with the school's technology coordinator to see if the coordinator knows anything about the product
d. Ask the class if they have heard of the game and if they think the game would be helpful to them in class.

89. A teacher has concerns that a standardized test she is required to give does not accurately measure what it is designed to measure. The test claims to measure students' abilities to make inferences, yet there are no questions that directly address this skill. The teacher has concerns with which aspect of the standardized test?

    a. Validity
    b. Reliability
    c. Bias
    d. Objectivity

90. In your second-year French class, many of your students expressed surprise at how poor their grades were on the mid-term progress report. The grades in your class are calculated according to a very simple formula, a large part of which comes from the grades given on daily work. Which strategy would best ensure that your students remain aware of their grades?

    a. Require the students to keep a running average of their daily grades in the front of their notebooks
    b. Post a list of student grades every week on the bulletin board organized by student ID number
    c. Send home a mini-report card every two weeks that the parents must sign
    d. Explain your grading system to the students one more time, and then leave it up to them

91. Two ESL students in the same class come from two countries with a long history of political, territorial, and religious conflicts. They already know one another personally. Neither student has formed an unfavorable opinion of the other prior to their acquaintance. Neither makes generalizations about the other's cultural attributes. The problem is rather that each student views his culture as superior to the other's. In developing a culturally responsive classroom environment, their teacher especially targets reducing _____ to decrease cultural bias in these two students.

    a. Prejudice
    b. Stereotyping
    c. Ethnocentrism
    d. All these factors

92. For students who have difficulty finishing routine assignments, the teacher should do all of the following except:

    a. Teach self-discipline about staying on task.
    b. Avoid playing games with the materials because they might add too much time to the task.
    c. Remove segments of the task; for example, don't require the student to copy word problems before calculating the answer.
    d. Divide the task into segments and allow the student to work on the parts throughout the day.

93. What is the most productive order to structure a class period?

    a. Seatwork, class discussion, content development
    b. Class discussion, seatwork, content development
    c. Seatwork, content development, class discussion
    d. Content development, class discussion, seatwork

94. Which of the following characteristics accurately describes authentic assessment techniques?

    a. They are norm-referenced
    b. They are designed to build higher-order thinking skills
    c. They allow students to choose from a set of teacher-prepared responses
    d. They measure students' performance at a specific point in time

95. Suppose that you are transitioning from one activity to another during class, but you notice that two of your students are still struggling to finish with the current task. What is the best recourse?

    a. Single the students out in front of the rest of the class so that they will feel more motivated to work better
    b. Do not go forward with the new activity and have the rest of the class wait while the two students finish their work
    c. Continue with the new activity, but allow the two students to continue and finish the activity they are on. Let them know quietly that they can meet with you after class to learn whatever they missed.
    d. Give the two students an *F* for the day since they did not finish their work on time

96. Which type of classroom environment is more likely to help more students to learn?

    a. One that focuses on order.
    b. One that is pleasant and comfortable.
    c. One that has classical music playing in the background.
    d. One that is broken up into sections that appeal to different types of personalities.

97. During a class discussion, a teacher has posed a question to her class, but no student has responded. What should she do?

    a. Continue to wait until a student answers
    b. Repeat the question
    c. Rephrase the question
    d. Tell the students the answer

98. Which learning theory is based on the idea that students are actively involved in constructing their own meaning, and that teachers should guide students through scaffolding rather than using instructor-led teaching techniques?

    a. Behaviorism
    b. Cognitivism
    c. Constructivism
    d. Social learning theory

99. Which strategy works better for keeping students from losing focus during longer talks or explanations?

    a. Break your lecture up with jokes or personal anecdotes
    b. Put a general outline of what you will discuss on the board
    c. Stop every minute or two and quiz a student at random on whether they understood the concept you are discussing
    d. Start off your lesson by asking the students what they already know about the subject

100. When students disagree during a class discussion, what should the teacher do to resolve the disagreement so that the class can proceed in an organized fashion?

a. Immediately tell the class what the correct answer is and move on
b. Encourage the students to work out their differences through a logical and friendly debate
c. Tell the students that whenever there is a disagreement in class, the student who is right will get extra credit
d. Discourage the students from disagreeing with each other in class, and instead have them ask you when they have a question

101. After examining the assessment results for their incoming class of students, the teachers determine that about 35% of the students do not meet grade level standards for math. Which of the following approaches would be most likely to improve the overall performance of the class on future tests?

a. Having the underperforming students take math class three extra times per week, while reducing the number of math classes that students who exceeded the math standard take per week by three
b. Having all students take an extra three periods of math, while reducing science classes to only two times per week
c. Creating a compulsory after-school remediation program for the students who are behind in math
d. Finding creative ways to incorporate math instruction into other subject areas, and offering optional math tutoring during lunch and after school

102. There are differences among planned activities that are necessary classroom routines, activities that are fun and provide a break, and activities that are directly related to the curriculum. Of the following, which is an activity for taking a break?

a. Singing a song.
b. Packing up to go home.
c. Playing math games.
d. Taking a field trip.

103. Acceptable use policies for school computers are intended to:

a. Deter students and school employees from accessing inappropriate information or engaging in illegal activities using school computers
b. Ensure that students and teachers do not accidentally stumble upon inappropriate material while using school computers
c. Teach students about copyright laws and plagiarism
d. Prevent students from transferring documents created on school computers to their home computers

104. Suppose you are holding a class discussion of current events in your 8th grade social studies class. What is the most effective way to get the quieter students to participate in the discussion?

a. Ask the more active students to stop raising their hands
b. Penalize students who do not participate in the discussion
c. Periodically ask questions directly to the quiet students
d. Offer extra credit to the students who participate the most

105. A math teacher notices that his English learner is silent in class and often has a hard time answering when called upon. Aware that sometimes silence in his culture can mean respect rather than regret or embarrassment, he decides not to call on him in class. Before making this accommodation, what should the teacher do first?

    a. Determine whether he feels that way about silence
    b. Speaking to his counselor to determine his motivation
    c. Consult with other teachers who have this student
    d. Reading more about this student's culture

106. Each year, Mr. Caldwell holds a debating contest in his language arts class. He does not tell the students which side of the argument they will be debating until the day of the debate, so the students must prepare to argue both sides. Which of the following best describes why this is a useful exercise?

    a. Practicing argumentation helps promote students' growing sense of autonomy
    b. Public speaking improves students' self-esteem and assertiveness
    c. Preparing to argue both sides of the debate develops students' higher-order thinking skills by promoting awareness of competing viewpoints
    d. Researching both sides of the argument develops students' organizational skills

107. Ms. Fry, a science teacher, gives her class verbal instructions about how to complete an experiment, but when she tells them to begin, the students do not seem to know what to do. Which of the following methods would have been least effective in communicating the directions more clearly?

    a. Asking the students to write down the instructions
    b. Asking students questions throughout her explanation to make sure that they were comprehending the directions
    c. Providing written instructions
    d. Asking students if they had any questions after she had explained the directions

108. Regarding immigrants and education, what does the law set by the Supreme Court decision *Plyler v. Doe* (1982) mandate?

    a. Schools can ask students and/or their parents about the immigration status of students.
    b. Schools can require proof of student documentation or try to document student status.
    c. Schools can deny immigrant students access if their immigrant status is undocumented.
    d. Schools can and must admit undocumented children due to their right to an education.

109. ESL students need knowledge in multiple areas to attain good English reading comprehension. Using English fairy tales like Goldilocks and the Three Bears or the Three Little Pigs, for example, and knowing that it is considered bad manners to steal porridge best reflects which type of knowledge?

    a. Knowledge of narrative structures
    b. Knowledge of cultural conventions
    c. Knowing grammar and vocabulary
    d. Knowledge of general information

110. A teacher is working with a group of third graders at the same reading level. Her goal is to improve reading fluency. She asks each child in turn to read a page from a book about mammal young. She asks the children to read with expression. She also reminds them they don't need to stop between each word; they should read as quickly as they comfortably can. She cautions them, however, not to read so quickly that they leave out or misread a word. The teacher knows the components of reading fluency are:

   a. Speed, drama, and comprehension
   b. Cohesion, rate, and prosody
   c. Understanding, rate, and prosody
   d. Rate, accuracy, and prosody

111. Which of the following would be a mistake when writing a criterion for an objective?

   a. Setting performance standards high enough to meet skills expectations.
   b. Setting realistic standards and time limits to avoid frustration.
   c. Gradually increasing expectations of accuracy as time goes by.
   d. Setting no limit to time or amount so that students are not pressured.

112. Mrs. Hanson gives a brief lecture and asks students to discuss a list of questions in pairs before the class as a whole discusses them. This technique is effective for facilitating class discussion primarily because:

   a. It gives students the opportunity to try out their answers in a "safe" environment before stating them in front of the class
   b. It encourages students to compare their answers to those of their classmates and revise them if they are not socially acceptable
   c. It develops students' higher-order thinking skills by demonstrating that there are differing perspectives
   d. It provides Mrs. Hanson with the opportunity to see which questions are most interesting to the students before the classroom-wide discussion commences

113. Which of the following is an example of teachers failing to communicate effectively with their students or other teachers?

   a. The students know the lesson's objective.
   b. Assignments for 5th graders are less demanding than those for 3rd graders in the same school.
   c. All 5th grade science classes are working on photosynthesis at the same time.
   d. Students have been provided with a grading rubric for their compositions.

114. How can a teacher end a lesson so that the students begin to process the material and keep it in their minds?

   a. Take a moment to talk about how the day's lesson connects and fits in with previous lessons and or the next day's lesson
   b. Give a pop quiz
   c. Call on a student at random to stand up before the class and explain what the most important thing he or she learned was
   d. Be sure that the students have a homework assignment every single day

115. Which of the following assessment methods would be most useful for fostering middle school students' ownership of their learning?

a. Providing students with charts showing their improvement over the course of a year
b. Giving the students pre- and post-tests for each instructional unit so that they can see their learning progress
c. Giving students detailed feedback on their performance and providing opportunities to incorporate the feedback and demonstrate improvement
d. Creating an environment wherein students openly compete to achieve the best grades, but are also rewarded for improvement

116. How can a teacher best ensure that a lesson will be coherent and logical?

a. Plan out the lesson in writing ahead of time
b. Ask the class every day if they understand
c. Make sure that your lesson never strays from the textbook
d. Rely on the sample lesson plans from the teacher's guidebook

117. Mr. Rogers is working with a diverse high school student body. He invites his students to articulate their widely varied perspectives, gives them debating and role-playing exercises to practice seeing others' viewpoints, and assists them in expressing their emotions as well as teaching them English language use and academic subject content. For which goal are his practices most relevant?

a. Recognizing, understanding, analyzing, and alleviating cultural identity crises
b. Decreasing conflicts among students from lack of intercultural understanding
c. Working with multicultural students to improve their academic achievements
d. Acknowledging the linguistic diversity among his students and addressing this

118. What is the best way to handle current events that are relevant to your class?

a. Keep your lesson plans flexible, and integrate extended discussions of current events as they occur.
b. Don't allow current events to distract the class. Keeping to your schedule is more important
c. Have students research current events on their own for extra credit
d. Set strict parameters on the discussion of current events, such as holding such discussion during the last ten minutes of class on Fridays.

119. In preparation for the upcoming school year, the test results shared with the teachers who will be working with the students the following year. How will this information be most useful to the students' new teachers?

a. It will determine which students should be placed in remedial classes
b. It will help the teachers plan their instruction based on the strengths and needs of the incoming students
c. It will help determine which students should repeat a grade
d. It will help the teachers decide whether or not they should use team teaching

120. What common misconception often makes it difficult to keep parents closely involved with their children's school life at the middle and high school levels?

    a. Many parents mistakenly believe that by high school, that their child's scholastic abilities have already been established, and so there is little point in parent involvement.
    b. Many parents mistakenly believe that their input is not welcomed by the school and teachers.
    c. Many parents mistakenly believe that being more involved at school will humiliate their child.
    d. Many parents mistakenly believe that becoming less involved in a child's school life will encourage the child to mature and become more responsible.

121. Which of the following options best describes the use of environmental print in a prekindergarten classroom?

    a. Including real food packages and menus in the dramatic play area
    b. Setting aside 10 minutes each day for students to read books independently
    c. Displaying sight words on a word wall
    d. Creating anchor charts of vocabulary words from content areas

122. Mr. Tollison has noticed that many of his eighth grade math students are not completing their homework assignments at all, are partially completing them or are completing the wrong problems. Mr. Tollison's first response should be to:

    a. Call the students' parents if they fail to turn in more than one assignment
    b. Grade whatever problems the students do turn in, even if they are not the right ones
    c. Develop a system to ensure that all students correctly record the homework assignment
    d. Walk the students through a few of the homework problems before they leave class

123. Which strategy should a history teacher use to get students more involved in the subject?

    a. Supplement the standard textbook with a variety of less academic materials, including narratives, biographies, and news articles from the time
    b. Have students read from the textbook out loud in class
    c. Make all of the class test questions essay questions
    d. Have students act out battles in the classroom

124. Which of the following describes a situation that should prompt a teacher to make an initial contact with a student's parents?

    a. After getting a *D* on her midterm, Sarah failed to turn in her class project, which counts for 20 percent of her grade.
    b. During the first week of class, you twice had to ask Brad to stop whispering to the girl sitting next to him.
    c. Since the beginning of class a few weeks ago, Kristen often comes to class dressed inappropriately, wearing bikini bottoms and tee shirts with messages that border on being offensive.
    d. During first few weeks of the quarter, Rick made excellent grades on his weekly German vocabulary test. However, for the last two weeks his scores have steadily dropped. He also seems to be gloomier than usual.

125. Which of the following statements are true of rubrics?

a. Rubrics are only useful for complex assignments like oral presentations and research papers
b. Rubrics must include at least three but no more than five categories
c. Rubrics are effective assessment tools because they provide students with more specific feedback
d. Both B and C are true

126. What is the best starting point for deciding on the floor plan of your classroom?

a. Make sure that all student desks are oriented with their backs to the windows, so as to ensure that no students will become distracted by events going on outside
b. Consider the size and shape of the room and decide where the optimal position would be for you to carry out most of your instruction
c. Arrange student desks so that they all face the chalkboard
d. Use whatever arrangement is already there. School administrators spend a lot of time before the beginning of the school year optimizing the floor plans of every classroom in the building.

127. After you send a student to the principal's office for repeatedly disrupting your class, the principal suspends the student for three days. Following the suspension, the principal informs you that he would like to put the student back in your class. What are your obligations?

a. You should do as instructed, and allow the student back into class.
b. You are not obligated to allow the student back into your class if you feel uncomfortable.
c. You must file a petition with the board of education if you do not want the student back in your class.
d. You have to let the student back in your class only if you cannot find another teacher willing to take the student.

128. Mrs. Li is a general education teacher in an inclusion classroom where several students have learning disabilities in writing. To assess her students' reading comprehension skills, Mrs. Li asks them to write in their journals for 15 minutes each day after a period of sustained, silent reading. However, she's concerned that the learning disabled students will become frustrated with this timed writing assignment. How should Mrs. Li handle this dilemma?

a. She should ask the learning disabled students to write as much as they can during the 15 minute period, although they probably won't be able to completely convey their thoughts
b. She should let the learning disabled students continue to read during the writing period
c. She should take the learning disabled students to a quiet area and facilitate a 15 minute group reading discussion while the other students write
d. She should tell the students to start their journal entries during class, and finish them up for homework

129. A school has always had a no hat or headwear rule in its dress code policy. Recently, an immigrant from Iran who wears religious head garb enrolled in the school. The school allowed for her to wear something on her head as an exception to the policy but still maintained no headwear in other situations. What effect does this MOST likely have for the student?

a. The student will feel special and unique because she is allowed to wear religious head garb.
b. The student may feel different and singled out, creating an environment in the school that is not accepting of differences.
c. The student will be indifferent to this because at least she is able to wear her head garb.
d. The student may feel it is unfair toward other students that they also cannot wear anything on their heads and begin protesting.

130. Which of the following would be an unethical use of school property?

    a. Mr. Jackson takes home a school-owned laptop because there is publishing software installed on it that will help him prepare handouts for class.
    b. Mrs. Wallenstein goes to the school supply room and takes a box of colored chalk to use for drawing pie charts on the board for his math class.
    c. Mr. Calhoun uses his classroom after school to sell Girl Scout cookies for his daughter.
    d. Mr. Martinov asks the school secretary to requisition a laser pointer for his lectures.

Answer Key and Explanations

1. B: Reading about life in a different country would be the best example of an activity that prompt students to explore educational content from varied and integrated perspectives. Other examples of such activities are those that encourage students to explore different viewpoints, learn through thematic units and work in study teams.

2. B: Bulletin boards are a great way to make your classroom more appealing to students and can also be a useful way to communicate rules, schedules, and other information. However, it is not absolutely essential that the bulletin boards be perfect on the first day of school. Answer A is much more important since students must have a good view of the main teaching area and if you have to move them around, it will make it harder for you to learn their names. Answer C is essential so that all students have access to the materials necessary for the class. Of course, this is not as critical with materials that will not be used until later in the term. Answer D is equally important if you intend to rely on these items in your teaching.

3. D: A sudden decline in academic performance could be caused by any of the factors listed. Certain eating disorders can cause declines in academic performance because of physical symptoms like lethargy and the students' attendant lack of motivation. Drug use can also cause lethargy, inattentiveness, and/or hyperactivity that can affect schoolwork. Parental divorce can cause depression and inability to focus, which can also contribute to a decline in academic achievement. However, it is important to remember that these problems do not always cause declines in academic achievement. Joining a sports team may cause sudden change in a student's life, causing them to need to adjust to perform well in both sporting and academic pursuits. Once the student is adjusted, participation in a school sports team should not cause problems with academics, and in fact, may reinforce study habits if the team requires the student to achieve a certain grade point average.

4. B: The theory suggests that some students learn better through verbal interaction, while others are more visual, physical, or artistic. By using a variety of teaching methods, rather than just lecturing or working problems on a chalkboard, a teacher will help ensure that more students will grasp a given topic. Any of these methods may be applied in the teaching of any subject.

5. C: Having each student write out his own step-by-step instructions will help them visualize the process in their minds and make them feel more confident about what they are doing. During the actual lab session, the students will also find it helpful to have the procedure spelled out in their own words. Answer A will do little if anything to calm their nerves, and nothing to help them learn about the process. Answer B will likely only make the students more nervous and more likely to make mistakes, since they will feel rushed. Answer D is not a bad idea except that with so many people talking in one classroom, it may be a bit chaotic.

6. B: The lesson plans for an experienced teacher do not have to be as detailed as they should be for a new teacher because some actions become second nature to a teacher after a while and go without saying. The steps to writing a good lesson plan do not vary with the teaching model but are the backbone of every lesson. The lesson opening, body, and closing do not need to be written in order; in fact, it is often best to write the body of the lesson first so that the teacher has had a chance to thoroughly think through the lesson before deciding on an appropriate opening. Since the lesson plan has a set pattern, all parts must be written, including pre-planning steps and editing tasks, not just the parts that will be presented to the students.

7. C: ELL students at the Beginning proficiency level in Listening have difficulty understanding even simple conversations on familiar topics (a), even with slowed speech, other verbal cues, and gestures and other linguistic supports (b). When they do not understand spoken English, they are more likely to observe others to glean cues but not request clarifications than vice versa (d).

8. D: Although all of the skills listed are part of digital literacy, the main focus of this assignment is to create writing on the same topic for two very different audiences. Students will therefore need to know how to adjust the formality of their writing so that it is appropriate for each audience. A post on the school website, which will be seen by numerous community members, should use a more formal tone than an email to a friend. Therefore, choice D is the most relevant skill for this particular assignment.

9. A: This approach clearly communicates the problem, while at the same time showing respect for the student. Additionally, it invites input from the parents. This is a very good way to lay the groundwork for a cooperative discussion. Answer B needlessly compares Mike's performance to the other students in the class, and worse yet, it offers no solution. Answer C would likely put the parents on the defensive since it questions whether they are helping Mike. Answer D does not effectively communicate the seriousness of the problem. The parents will leave the meeting thinking that it's no big deal.

10. B: Vocabulary. Strategizing in order to understand the meaning of a word, knowing multiple meanings of a single word, and applying background knowledge to glean a word's meaning are all ways in which an effective reader enhances vocabulary. Other skills include an awareness of word parts and word origins, the ability to apply word meanings in a variety of content areas, and a delight in learning the meanings of unfamiliar words.

11. A: IDEA requires schools to provide learning disabled students with a free and appropriate education, even if the student has been suspended or expelled from school for disciplinary reasons. Since some students have disabilities that cause them to misbehave, refusing to educate them on this basis would constitute discrimination. C is not correct because the IDEA requires learning disabled students to be educated in the least restrictive environment possible, so many students are taught wholly or partly in general education classrooms with non-disabled students. D is incorrect because schools are required to pay for accommodations for learning disabled students.

12. B: "Know" might be appropriate for a general goal or standard, but is not a measurable action. The teacher cannot know if a student truly comprehends or has learned something unless there is a demonstration of the knowledge. The behavior component of an objective states what students will do to demonstrate their learning. Thus, this component is written as an observable verb so that the outcome can be measured. Calculate, define, and predict all ask the students to do a specific, concrete task, probably written. These verbs command an action.

13. B: Since fourth graders are in the concrete operational stage of development, they grasp concepts best through hands-on, concrete explanations. Showing that multiplying two fractions together produces a fraction of a fraction and demonstrating this using manipulatives would be more effective than verbal explanations. While answer A might also be effective, this exercise simply convinces students of the truth of the assertion, rather than showing them why it is true.

14. D: All of the listed options can assist students with developing reading skills, and students will have individual opinions regarding preferred activities. However, reading is a social experience that helps children learn about themselves and the world around them. Using language creatively, such as through rhyming, helps them understand all of the ways that language can be used. Reading and discussing stories together is also a social experience that connects readers and makes them part of a community of learners. These benefits will likely contribute to a love of reading more than practicing isolated skills.

15. B: Teachers are legally and ethically required to keep student records confidential (a) and also to protect the privacy of any or all student personal information. By copyright law, teachers are legally required both to seek and get permission (c) from either authors or publishers (d) to utilize copyrighted materials as teaching resources.

16. D: Assimilation is the process in which an individual tries to adopt the culture of the dominant culture and rejects his or her culture. Accommodation is a process in which members of the mainstream culture and the minority culture both learn to adapt to one another. Biculturalism is when an individual is able to function in two different cultures. Culture shock occurs once the initial excitement of being in a new culture wears off and the individual feels frustrated by the confusion and differences between the two cultures.

17. A: A lesson-planning matrix makes it easier for teachers to plan their lessons around a variety of useful strategies. Answer B does not take into account how one will incorporate the students' various skills into lesson. Moreover, students are not always fully aware of their learning abilities. Answer C fails to address lesson planning at all, and also might make the slower students feel that they are being unfairly singled out. Answer D is in fact one way to improve the comprehension of some students, but it is only one method, and will not especially help students who are not visually oriented.

18. B: Studies have shown that no other factor affects a student's performance in school as much as the degree to which the student's family is involved in his or her life. All of the other factors listed also have their influence too, but if a student's family takes an active interest in the student's performance in school, the other factors are more likely to be overcome, and the student's grades, attitude, and likelihood of graduation are all likely to be higher. Whatever a teacher can to encourage this is to the student's advantage.

19. C: An offense involving a sexual misconduct is serious and should immediately be referred to the principal's office. If the situation is out of control, then the police should also be contacted. Answer A, detention, is not a severe enough punishment. Answer B is unlawful. Answer D, corporal punishment, is also not within a teacher's authority. For offenses this serious, the teacher should do what is necessary to end the situation, and then refer the problem to the principal or vice principal. In such cases, punishment is not the teacher's responsibility.

20. D: While all of these causes may contribute to the class' behavior, the most important reason for it is that middle school students, especially sixth-graders, tend to be anxious about completing transitions. Since students at this level are not used to changing classes, doing so within the allotted time makes them anxious and they want to be as prepared as possible by packing up their belongings. Mrs. Brown could effectively combat this behavior by assuring students that they will have plenty of time to get to their next class, and allowing a few minutes at the end of the class for the students to prepare for the transition.

21. C: It is inappropriate for a teacher to directly approach a student and ask them about any disability they may have. This could be interpreted as harassment. A student may volunteer this information if he or she likes, or a teacher may approach the student's guidance counselor or the principal with such concerns, who may then contact the parents and recommend a medical consultation, but it is not a teacher's job to attempt to diagnose any such condition.

22. B: Allowing students to pick their own groups defeats the purposes outlined above and will most likely result in groups that were chosen by the students so that they could be with friends rather than good working partners. Flexible grouping is designed to put students together in groups that work well for various purposes. One type of group would be one in which the students can work according to similar interests. Others would group students according to readiness levels or specific skill levels. In other words, the grouping would be teacher-selected according to assessments that indicate the needed diversity or similarities to make the group efficient.

23. C: Constructivism is a learning theory based on the idea that people are actively involved in the learning process, rather than being passive receivers of knowledge. Constructivism suggests that children learn best by solving real-world problems, gathering information, testing ideas, and other active processes, with teachers guiding and scaffolding them along the way.

24. B: The placement of computer workstations is dictated by the location of electrical outlets and Internet connections. Therefore it is highly desirable to arrange their location before bringing in other equipment. Answer A, the teacher's desk, is less critical, but should be positioned so that it affords the teacher a good view of the classroom when the teacher is working. Answer C, filing cabinets, are the least critical item, and may usually be left until last, since the only issues concerning their placement are that they should be out of the way of student traffic and should be easily accessible from the teacher's desk. Answer D, the overhead projector, needs to be position within a direct line of sight to the projection screen, but since these projectors are often on wheeled carts, they can be easily moved out of the way when not in use.

25. B: Since middle school students are so developmentally diverse, progress-focused assessment methods allow teachers to maintain high expectations while meeting students where they are academically. Progress-focuses assessment methods are not intended to "coddle" underachieving students (C and D), but rather to provide them with an opportunity to succeed academically despite having a starting point below grade-level expectations.

26. D: Behaviorism (the theory) and behavior modification (the practice) are confined to observable, quantifiable behaviors. This is based on the premise that only an individual's external behaviors, that is, what he or she does, can be observed, measured, and therefore changed by others. Behaviorism and behavior modification do not deny the existence of internal states like thoughts (A), sensory perceptions (B), or emotions (C); they simply exclude these from being recorded or manipulated by others because others cannot observe them. Behaviorism maintains that, what we cannot observe, we cannot reliably measure and thus cannot consistently manipulate or change.

27. C: Benji's behavior signals that he might be using illegal drugs. Students who begin using drugs may suddenly become more sluggish or more restless than usual, and they may begin experiencing abnormal sleep patterns that interfere with school attendance. A is incorrect because learning disabilities do not usually develop "overnight," unless they are caused by an accident or acute medical condition. Benji's symptoms also do not fit the symptoms of depression (D). Also, such rapid and detrimental changes are not normal, even for adolescents whose minds and bodies are changing rapidly (B).

28. B: Breaking the item in to smaller sections makes memorization much easier. Answer A is an important part of memorization, but without breaking a topic up into smaller sections, many students will have a hard time. Answer C is ineffective unless the student has a photographic memory. Playing music in the background is helpful to some, but later the student may have difficulty if the same music is not playing when the student tries to recall the subject matter.

29. C: Accommodation occurs when something challenges a person's existing schema and causes it to be altered. In choice C, the child has a negative opinion of bees until she learns the role that they play in pollination. Her schema is altered, and she now views them as helpful. The other options demonstrate examples of assimilation, which occurs when someone takes in new information and adds it to existing schema rather than changing it. In choice A, the student applies the information she knows about sentences to punctuate the question. In choice B, the student applies information about the writing process to a new type of text. In choice D, the child assumes that the tiger is a lion because it makes the same sound.

30. C: Ms. Schneider should take the paraprofessional aside and explain her concerns. She should attempt to find out what is causing the behavior, and help the paraprofessional find a way to improve his performance. She should only begin approaching others regarding the problem after she has discussed the problem directly with the paraprofessional and given him a chance to improve his performance.

31. A: As teens develop affectively, socially, and morally, adults can support their growth by helping them to plan ahead for situations involving peer pressure to engage in risky behaviors and/or involving their friends' risky behaviors. Helping them anticipate and plan is important as teens often encounter such situations for the first time. While experts advise adults to respect teen needs for privacy, they also advise adults to show interest in teenagers' activities (b). Although depression is common during adolescence, adults should ask them about any suicidal ideations (c) and other feelings, which can avert rather than precipitate tragedy. While adolescence involves many behavioral changes, adults should not attribute all of these to the life stage, but rather should investigate further (d) any marked changes in behavior causing concern.

32. B: Work with the student to come up with several acceptable options for solving the problems and ask the student to commit to one of them. It may also be helpful to involve the student's parents and or guidance counselor. The student is much more likely to cooperate if he has more than one option. Answer A will likely lead to more problems. Answer C might be a practical option depending on the school, but once more, the student will be more likely to respond constructively if there are multiple options. Answer D, like answer A, does not get at the root of the problem. Since this attitude is not typical of the student, it indicates a bigger problem.

33. D: If you are overwhelmed and losing control of your class, it is very important that you step forward and ask for help promptly, rather than allowing things to keep getting worse. Most of your colleagues will have had similar experiences and can help you find a workable solution. This is a challenge faced by nearly all new teachers, and they need to be able to ask for help when they need it. Answer A is too risky. While any teacher needs time to adjust and adapt to new challenges, this should not be done at the expense of the students. They are not guinea pigs. Answer B is unfair. You have already established that the problem is not with the students. It is with you. Answer C is absurd. There is no such thing as an "easy class." Each one has its challenges. You will not impress your principal and colleagues by giving up.

34. A: According to Vygotsky, activities in the zone of proximal development are ones that students are almost able to complete independently, but they require some scaffolding. The activities are not too easy or too difficult, but just challenging enough to allow some growth to occur. Reading books at the instructional level with teacher guidance is an example of an activity in the zone of proximal development. Choices B and D represent activities that are easy for the student. Choice C demonstrates a way to make a text accessible for a student when it is too difficult for the student to read independently.

35. C: Educators may legally accept gifts that are offered openly by students, parents, supervisors, etc., provided these gifts are offered to recognize or express appreciation for the educator's service. Gifts that influence an educator's professional judgment are prohibited. The code prohibits educators from interfering with the political rights of their colleagues, deceiving others with regard to the policies of the school district or educational institution, and revealing confidential student information (unless the disclosure is for a lawful professional purpose or is required by law).

36. C: The moment when you first observe a detrimental pattern forming in the student's behavior or schoolwork is the time to bring the parents into the picture. Answers A and B are somewhat impractical. Both teachers and parents have very limited time. Moreover, if you contact the parents too often, parents may not take you as seriously. Answer D is waiting too late. Once a problem becomes extreme, it becomes much more difficult to solve.

37. B: This graphic organizer could be used to help the student identify the main elements of the story, including the characters, problem, plot, and resolution. Therefore, it could be used to help the student summarize the story. It does not contain any prompts requiring the student to use the higher-level thinking skills required to infer, draw conclusions, or evaluate.

38. D: An overhead projector is by far the most effective way to display information for a class if the chalkboard is unavailable for use. Answer A is a sure way to annoy your fellow teachers. Just because you are floating does not mean that the other teacher using the room is floating too. Answer B might be okay for college teaching, but is unacceptable in a secondary school environment. Answer C presumes that all students have access to a computer and printer at home, which may not always be the case.

39. A: The teacher needs to know how well each student is doing and must teach each child. The teacher is striving for a quality learning experience for every child rather than averages or high percentages measured by a group-wide evaluation. It is true that evaluation must be part of every lesson, in some form or another, or else the teacher will not know if the objective was reached, and if some or all students need a re-teach. This evaluation can continue with retention checks in other lessons; that is, on an on-going basis, and may be repeated in overall unit tests.

40. B: When resolving behavior problems, teachers should strive to be consistent and objective (B). Consistency is important because students will not feel that they are being singled out and treated differently than other students, and objectivity is key because practicing it will prevent the teacher's own biases from affecting his or her students. Together, objectivity and consistency will help the teacher run the classroom fairly and earn students' respect. A is incorrect because teachers should avoid reacting judgmentally to behavior. This can aggravate behavior problems with students who conclude that the teacher just "doesn't like" them or "doesn't understand" them. While patience and collaboration maybe useful in dealing with behavior problems, they are not as important as consistency and objectivity because being patient and/or collaborative alone does not provide a mode for directly addressing the behavior (i.e., one could be patient and collaborative but still inconsistent and ineffective at solving the behavior problem).

41. A: Mr. Aaron should give all students in the group the opportunity to confidentially rate the contributions of their fellow group members, and give lower grades to students who are rated lower by the members of their group. This approach will give each student an incentive to contribute equally, because they can receive a lower grade if they do not contribute. This method would allow Mr. Aaron to grade fairly in cases where certain students fail to contribute.

42. B: The FERPA stipulates that parents of children under 18 can inspect and request amendments to their children's educational records on demand (B). However, once students reach the age of majority, they become "eligible students." This means that this right is transferred to them and their permission is required to disclose their educational records to anyone, including their parents. Written permission from parents or the eligible student is not required in order to disclose records to a school official with a legitimate educational interest (C) or to a school to which the student is transferring (D).

43. B: Research finds that, when children begin school with language deficiencies, it is because their home and community settings and peer groups do not provide sufficient support or opportunities for language development. Language deficits are NOT found to prevail among certain socioeconomic groups (A), cultural backgrounds (C) or ESL/ELL children (D). Researchers point out that children from wealthy families can be deficient in language skills as well as those from poor families and that ESL/ELL children can excel in English at school just as native English-speaking children can perform below average scholastically. The prevalence of language deficits in ESL/ELL settings is more due to many of these children's English exposure being limited to school lessons.

44. B: When children reach the preoperational stage, they begin to think symbolically. At this point, they are able to begin understanding the relationship between letters (symbols) and sounds, also known as the alphabetic principle. Children are typically in the sensorimotor stage until about age 2, and they are not yet able to think symbolically in this stage. The concrete operational stage lasts from ages 7 to 12, and the formal operational stage lasts from age 12 until adulthood.

45. D: Experts advise classroom teachers to avoid using slang and idiomatic expressions when teaching ELLs with language learning disabilities. Though these students will eventually need to understand some idioms, teachers should not employ them initially with ESL students having concomitant language LDs. Experts do advise classroom teachers to model frequently (A) for these students; to speak more slowly (B); and to use multisensory/multimodal teaching methods (C).

46. C: Offering students an option of formats for class projects is a great way to take advantage of both new technologies and of multiple intelligence theory. Some students are much more likely to succeed by doing a video project or a blog than a traditional written report. Moreover, students will need to know how to use these technologies after graduation anyway. Some students will do far better creating a video than a paper. However, it is very important that the teacher verifies that content is substantive and of high quality, regardless of the format in which the project is completed. Teachers should also be competent enough with the available technologies that they know how to guard against plagiarism.

47. A: In the pre-alphabetic stage of word learning, children do not yet have an understanding of letter/sound relationships they can use to decode words. They may remember some words based on visual features, such as words found in environmental print. Choice B describes the partial alphabetic stage, when children begin to use letter/sound relationships to decode some sounds in words, particularly the beginning and ending sounds. Choice C describes the full alphabetic stage, and choice D describes the consolidated alphabetic stage.

48. B: If a teacher corrects ESL students every single time they make any kind of mistake (A), many of them would feel so inhibited they would be afraid to say anything. Many grammatical errors do not significantly interfere with communication. While serious errors should be corrected, teachers do better to make notes of these and then point them out after a class activity is over rather than interrupting the activity's/discussion's flow. Teachers should also make use of student errors to inform themselves of further student learning needs when they plan additional practice for the class (C). Rather than only highlighting errors, teachers should equally acknowledge good work at expressing ideas in English with encouraging words (D) during oral activities, and with check marks or similar written feedback on written assignments.

49. D: Although copying definitions might help to cement the meaning of a word, if the word is not one that is relevant to the lesson, it will be quickly forgotten. Answer D violates the guideline that practicing skills should be embedded within application opportunities and is busy-work practice with no point to the effort. Reading does help students to improve word attack skills, as well as many other skills, so Answer A is a worthwhile objective. If the objective is to improve number facts and computations, solving problems is a good practice, so Answer B is also a worthwhile objective. In the process of writing an essay, the student has to practice spelling and penmanship skills, so this assignment achieves a good objective, as stated in Answer C.

50. C: A scaled score is most useful for comparing students' performance across different administrations of the same test. (For example, comparing this year's sixth graders to last year's, or comparing the performance of students at different schools who took different versions of the same test. Raw scores simply indicate the number of questions a student answered correctly (A), and can only be used to compare students' performance on that specific version of the assessment.

51. B: The cultural incompatibility theory is the belief that the difference between home and school culture leads to lower academic success in students. Neither culture is seen as right or wrong, but instead, the values are "mismatched." This has put the onus on teachers to change the conditions in the classroom to accommodate for all students' cultures; however, the result has been that schools continue the status quo with the expectation placed on the home culture adapting to the school culture. Although the goal was to foster multicultural perspective and an understanding of different cultures, ultimately the cultural incompatibility theory has not positively impacted schools' abilities to support English learners.

52. A: This objective is generic enough to emphasize knowledge and skills that would apply in a variety of situations – knowledge about science fiction and fantasy helps to evaluate a large number of reading selections. The content of an objective should be specific enough that anyone reading it will understand the subject matter. The content should be able to stand alone and be understood without having to look up specific materials; consequently, answer B is not a good example of content because it refers to specific materials -- Unit 6 in the vocabulary book. In like manner, answer D refers to specific materials (p. 114 in the textbook). The content should also be generic enough that the emphasis is on knowledge and skills that are applicable in a number of contexts; answer C is not generic enough but could be fixed by adding the skills that would be learned from the task.

53. A: Establishing a clear set of rules for your classroom from the very beginning is the best way to let your students know what is expected of them. Giving the students the rules in writing ensures that they have no excuse to not know what the rules are. Answer B works for some teachers, but not for all. Moreover, it is not necessarily to your advantage to establish yourself in a negative light before your students. Answer C is a very bad idea. Waiting to establish the rules will likely result in chaos, and students will get the idea that they can get away with anything. Answer D is also unhelpful. Your rules should be consistent. Changing them often will confuse your students, and might cause them to take your rules less seriously.

54. A: Euphoria is the initial stage that individuals generally experience due to the excitement of being a new culture. Cultural fatigue and culture shock are the same stage in which newcomers are disoriented and frustrated by the difference between cultures. The final stage is adjustment, which is sometimes known as adaptation. This is when the individual adjusts to the new culture and is able to successfully integrate into the dominant culture.

55. D: Portfolios are collections of students' writing samples gathered over time. Students can review their writing samples and use observations, checklists, or rubrics to evaluate how their writing skills have evolved over time. Norm-referenced and criterion-referenced tests are both formal and standardized tests. Norm-referenced tests compare students' performances to the performances of sample groups of similar students. Criterion-referenced tests indicate whether or not students have mastered certain skills and identify which skills require additional instruction. Students write for authentic purposes when completing performance-based tasks, but these do not show growth over time.

56. C: Prekindergarten students are likely in the emergent stage of reading development, where they are developing an understanding of the concepts of print. In this stage, they are in the beginning stages of learning to recognize letters and letter/sound relationships. Therefore, an activity that focuses on letter identification is most developmentally appropriate. The other activities require more complex phonics skills and would be more appropriate for students in the early stage of reading development.

57. C: Incorporating self-assessment into the classroom is important because it prepares students for the future when they will need to evaluate their own work in the absence of an instructor.

58. A: Establish a firm routine, such as leading a roll call or reviewing the previous day's homework. When everyone knows exactly what to expect, and when to expect it, they will fall in with the routine as well. Answer B will result in the students taking even longer to settle down. Answer C is impractical and, unless you actually enforce it, will result in the students not taking you seriously. Answer D sets a very bad example and implies that good discipline is negotiable.

59. A: intrinsic motivation can be fostered by helping students to develop a personal connection to and interest in the material they're learning. Intrinsic motivation refers to a person's desire to do something (like a hobby) without any apparent material motivation and without any threat of punishment should the activity not be done. In contrast, answer B refers to extrinsic motivation. This type of motivation propels a person to do something not because they enjoy the activity for its own sake, but because they fear punishment or desire rewards produced by that activity.

60. A: The teacher should circulate around the room, but should avoid spending too much time with any one group since this tends to distract the teacher's attention from what is going on in other groups. Answer B is not important, although the teacher should be sure that all students cooperate effectively on the project. Answer C is the opposite of what the teacher should be doing. By circulating among the groups and taking notes, the teacher can help with problems, and verify that all students are actively participating. Answer D is a bad idea, since some students might work harder than others. Therefore the teacher needs to verify the degree to which the students are participating.

61. D: Piaget's theory posits four distinct stages of cognitive development, each with specific distinguishing characteristics and corresponding to approximate age ranges. Skinner's (A) theory of cognitive development is behavioral. It does not include stages but focuses on the premise that changes in behaviors over time represent learning and that this learning occurs through the antecedent and consequent events immediately before and after a behavior, which increase or decrease the probability of the individual's repeating the behavior. Vygotsky's (B) theory also has no stages and focuses on sociocultural influences as sources of learning. Bandura's (C) social

Copyright © Mometrix Media. You have been licensed one copy of this document for personal use only. Any other reproduction or redistribution is strictly prohibited. All rights reserved.

learning theory has no stages either; it focuses on learning through observation, imitation of models, and vicarious learning.

62. C: Chomsky's theory proposes innate, "hard-wired" biological capacities like a Language Acquisition Device (LAD) and universal generative grammar enable children's language development. This supports the observation that children of all cultures develop language in the same stages and patterns around the same ages. Skinner's behaviorist theory, which emphasizes environmental influences (A), is less compatible: Children acquire language faster than they could through conditioning processes; they could not generate the infinite sentences possible via imitation; they learn without regular adult correction; and they overregularize irregular verbs without adult modeling. Whorf's linguistic relativity hypothesis (B) is also less compatible because Whorf proposed language differentially influences people's thinking by culture (e.g., Eskimo languages have far more words for snow than English). Neural networks (D) propose children learn similarly to computer systems with no preprogramming via exposure to many language examples. As this would vary among cultural contexts, it is also less compatible with universal language development than Chomsky's ideas.

63. A: Learner-centered assessment provides alternatives that allow different students to be assessed differently. Although student participation in assessment creation (D) is also an important part of learner-centered assessment, a multiple choice test does not reflect the goals of learner-centered assessment because it does not provide an authentic assessment experience.

64. B: In order to identify and resolve the problem, Mrs. Thomas' first step should be to consider whether there may be a problem with the assessment itself. Perhaps the assessment did not directly test the material that was covered, or perhaps the students were not given adequate time to complete the assessment. Only if Mrs. Thomas finds no problems with the test itself should she analyze the results to find out exactly which aspects of the material the students struggled with.

65. C: The best approach for a teacher in regards to using technology in the classroom is to use only the technology with which s/he is comfortable so that the technology does not complicate or distract from the lesson. Answer A is not the best approach because while the teacher should know enough to demonstrate the technology used in the classroom, it is not the teacher's job to teach technology; therefore, the teacher should not be hesitant to use technology out of fear of having to become a technical expert. Answer B is not the best approach because the teacher needs to find a balance between using the technology center and working with computers in the classroom. It is more convenient to stay in the classroom, but the technology center exists to expand capabilities. Answer D is not the best approach because while increasing technology might improve instruction, there is no guarantee; only better teaching can improve instruction.

66. B: Mr. Fields is most likely to achieve his objective by assigning nightly homework problems that are peer-graded in class the next day, and going over the answers after the assignment is graded. This method offers two advantages: first, students receive immediate feedback on their performance that they can begin to apply to future assignments and tests; second, students have the opportunity to find out why they arrived at wrong answers when the teacher goes over the problems. This makes assessment a positive experience that helps students perform better in the future, rather than making it a negative experience that de-motivates students by making them feel powerless to improve their performance.

67. C: The best option would be to refer the students to the school's peer mediation program. Peer mediation can be effective for resolving disputes among students, and would be preferable to separating the students because it would teach them to work through problems with peers. Answer

A is incorrect because there is no indication that the conflict is racial in nature, and D would not be effective because fighting between students is not something that cannot typically be accommodated through rule changes.

68. B: The number of unrecognizable words an English Language Learner encounters when reading a passage or listening to a teacher. Language load is one of the barriers English Language Learners face. To lighten this load, a teacher can rephrase, eliminate unnecessary words, divide complex sentences into smaller units, and teach essential vocabulary before the student begins the lesson.

69. C: Parents are generally more cooperative if they see that you are trying to work with them rather than against them. Answer A is unlikely to work. Fighting with parents usually only leads to making things worse. Answer B is equally unhelpful. If parents feel like you are avoiding them, they will likely approach the principal of your school, and create problems for you. There is some truth in Answer D. If you minimize the problem, parents will have a legitimate complaint. Nevertheless, the teacher still must be diplomatic and respectful if he or she hopes to make any progress toward a solution.

70. D: Having the students consider real life applications of math problems is a great way to help make the subject seem less abstract and more interesting. Answer A is an invitation to chaos, and also uses up a lot of class time. Answer B wastes even more class time. It is unfair to have the whole class wait while the teacher speaks individually with each student. Such a meeting should be held after class. Answer C may sometimes be useful, but probably not in this case. You have already determined that your students are bored, and repeating material will likely be even more boring for them.

71. A: The objective is like a public declaration for all to see – not only the students, but also other teachers, administrative staff, and parents who want to know what is going on that day and whether the objective has been clearly communicated to the students. One of the benefits of a clearly written, focused objective is that the teacher knows exactly what to evaluate – did the students learn the objective for the day? Another benefit is that the evaluation works in reverse also – providing a measure for the teacher to judge his/her own effectiveness. It is the primary purpose of an objective to focus the students on what they are to learn that day; in addition, a well-written objective might also motivate students to want to learn the day's lesson.

72. D: ELL students at the Advanced level of ELP for Listening and Speaking as mispronouncing words, but still speaking well enough that others unfamiliar with ELLs usually understand them. Students at this level speak grade-level English socially and academically comfortably, though with some pauses (a) for repetition, restatement, or word/phrase searches for clarification. They understand basic social conversations and academic discussions, but sometimes need others to repeat, rephrase, or slow down for clarification (b). They can use common abstract vocabulary, but still make errors with complex grammar (c) that impede communication somewhat.

73. C: This response describes the learning condition rather than the evaluation condition. Objectives focus on outcomes, not on when or where the students gain the knowledge; therefore, "after completing the unit on World War I" is not a good example of an evaluation condition. Describing the evaluation condition or conditions of an objective provides additional specificity about what the student will learn. The condition can affect the difficulty level of the objective and determine the lesson and practice activities. An evaluation condition should ask students to perform a skill in isolation or in context, tell students what information or materials will be provided, or describe the setting or situation involved in the objective. Answer A is an example of materials provided – on graph paper. Answer B is an example of a setting or situation – during partner practice. Answer D is an example of information provided – given a list of European countries.

74. C: Mr. Ferris can use the change-tracking device in Microsoft Word to show the students how to improve their papers. Answer D is not correct, because Mr. Ferris could still track grammatical errors if the reports were in paper form. Answers A and B are not correct because, although these are advantages, they are not as helpful for assessment purposes as answer C.

75. A: Experts recommend adult vigilance for signs of eating disorders in later adolescence, and awareness of and responsiveness to older teens' increasing concerns about post-secondary educational and career plans. They advise adults give adolescents support and advice, not strict rules and direction (b). They need a balance of structure and basic rules with freedom for exploration, experimentation, identity formation, and self-expression. Adults should not only point out but actually create opportunities for teens to use their developing problem-solving and conflict-resolution skills and judgment (c). Although many teens resist adult advice about healthful behaviors and are prone to risky behaviors, they are also very concerned about self-images, appearances, attractiveness, and energy for all their activities; adults can often interest them in healthy sleep, diet, and exercise habits by explaining how these support those areas of concern. Adults should not assume in advance that teens will not follow such advice (d).

76. A: At the very least, parents should have a list of the basic requirements of the class, including any term papers or long-term projects that the students will have to complete. Answer B is great if you have the time to put it together, but it is not essential. Answer C is probably more information than most parents really want. Answer D is simply unrealistic. Unfortunately, not all parents are willing or able to become experts in all of the subjects their children are studying.

77. A: of the practices described here, providing opportunities for students to work cooperatively with peers is most likely to promote a productive classroom environment for older elementary and middle-level students. The classroom environment should be planned and structured, as opposed to frequently changed (B), and students should be encouraged to work cooperatively, rather than independently (C). In addition, kinesthetic and active learning activities can be very beneficial for middle-level students (D).

78. C: Talking to your colleagues is the best way to catch up with the current trends. Of course you are under no obligation to copy them, but you may come away with some ideas to make your classroom more functional. Answer A is like sticking your head in the sand. You should always be open to new ideas. Answer B may cause you to miss out on understanding the reasons behind some of the new trends, and also if you copy other rooms too closely, your students may get the wrong idea about you. Answer D will not result in a classroom that serves your purposes. However, there is nothing wrong with asking a couple of your more artistic students to help you decorate, once you have decided what you want to do.

79. A: If Mr. Stratton's goal is to ensure that students understand what is expected of them and that they are able to complete the project on schedule, the best approach for him to take would be to explain how to do the research and set several 'checkpoints' before the final product is due. By explaining the research process, Mr. Stratton ensures that all students understand what they're expected to do. Setting checkpoints, (for example, asking students to submit a brief description of their project one month before it is due and asking them to submit a rough draft one week before it is due), Mr. Stratton can make sure that all of his students are on track to complete the project as scheduled.

80. C: By providing recent immigrant families with materials pertinent to the orientation in their native languages, the teachers will ensure that the families understand the content of the materials. Providing the families with a detailed analysis of the district ESL program (A) will not give them an understanding of all of the school's protocols and culture, but of only one component. Asking the ESL students to interpret for their families (B) does not acknowledge that many of these recent immigrant students may not have the English-language proficiency to interpret, and doing so could activate the students' affective filters. Arranging discussion groups about the families' native languages (D) can promote communication among these families, but it will not help students' parents understand the information the teachers are presenting to them during the orientation event.

81. C: Learning these skills early will help students to mature and become responsible adults. Answer A is hardly necessary. Most students find themselves under stress anyway. Answer B should not be an issue as long as the teacher is attentive and properly checks the students' work. Answer D is a very cynical viewpoint. While this may happen on occasion, such projects are still very much worthwhile.

82. B: effective rules are usually stated positively. Stating rules negatively, as in answer A or especially D, proscribe specific behaviors, but by definition "allow" all other behaviors not discussed. Further, it sends students the message that they are expected to misbehave, and makes positive reinforcement difficult. (It makes more sense to say, "Class, you can play for 15 minutes because you did an excellent job of working quietly today," than to say, "You did a good job of not yelling and bothering other students, so you may play outside"). While it may be appropriate to phrase rules politely (C), simply doing this does not have the same impact as stating them positively.

83. D: Validating cultural identities of the students is a great step toward creating a multicultural curriculum. It is important to distinguish between multiculturalism and globalism. Globalism refers to the cultures around the world, whereas multiculturalism focuses on different cultures within the United States. Although Answer A is an excellent strategy for schools to undertake, it promotes globalism rather than multiculturalism. Professional development is also another key aspect of changing a curriculum; however, Answer B focuses on technology rather than on teacher cultural self-reflection or understanding minority cultures in the United States. Guest speakers are also a great asset to building a multicultural curriculum, but these are often one-off events, which can be more surface level.

84. D: The individual teacher is ultimately responsible for keeping up with the latest ideas. The school system, the principal, and other teachers can often be excellent resources, and may even set up programs or continuing education requirements to help teachers stay current, but this does not always occur, and in any case, it remains a teacher's responsibility to ensure that his or her skills are constantly improving.

85. D: Using music and musical notation to explain the concept of fractions is a clear example of a lesson that follows the multiple intelligence theory. Students who are more musically inclined will find this kind of lesson especially useful. Answer A is the traditional way, and it does not employ multiple intelligence techniques. Answer B also has little to do with multiple intelligences. Answer C does not necessarily make use of multiple intelligences, though it could if the right examples were chosen.

86. C: Planning, above all else, will help a teacher ensure that a class will proceed smoothly. All to the other items will follow if a teacher exercises good planning skills.

87. C: Giving the students an active task, such as taking notes, will force the students to focus on the content of the tour. Answer A will do little to change or inspire the students to pay more attention. Answer B also has little to do with what students get out of the experience. Answer D is backwards. Having a quiz after the test would make more sense.

88. C: It might be a good idea, but it is best to do a little research first and talk to the technology coordinator. It is important to make sure that the game is truly educational, is practical for class use, and also that it is appropriate for use with the age group of the students in his class. Answer A is risky. At the very least the teacher should spend some time with the game and verify that it looks promising. Answer B is closed minded. After all, there are indeed some useful educational games that can successfully be used in class. Answer D is unreliable, since most students would be happy to play a game instead of listening to a lecture.

89. A: A test is valid if it measures what it is designed to measure. If a test claims to measure a student's ability to make inferences, then the questions on the test should require students to use this skill. Reliability refers to ensuring that there is consistency in test results over time and between participants. Bias refers to ensuring that the test does not put any participants at a disadvantage. Objectivity refers to ensuring that all tests are scored in the same manner without being affected by any outside influences or bias.

90. A: Requiring students to keep a running tally of their average in the front of their notebook will force them to think about their grade every day. It will also directly involve them in the process and teach them to be independently responsible about keeping up with their grades. Answer B is too passive, since some of the students would forget to check it. Answer C will be seen by some as overly invasive. It also lacks the advantages of teaching the students to keep track of their grades themselves. Answer D will be insufficient for many students.

91. C: Viewing one's culture as superior to others (and/or being unaware of other cultures) is a definition of ethnocentrism. The two students are described as having this view. They are described as not having prejudice (A) toward one another because they have not formed unfavorable opinions of one another prior to meeting. They are described as not stereotyping (B) one another because they do not make generalizations about one another's cultural attributes. Therefore, (D) is also incorrect.

92. B: It helps students to stick to a task if the task is made more fun by adding novelty to it through games or personal interest materials. For students who have difficulty staying with and completing routine tasks, the teacher can employ certain strategies that will encourage the child to stick with the work. One way is to explain to the students about the importance of remaining on-task and monitoring oneself. Another way is to eliminate any part of the routine that really isn't necessary, such as copying sentences. Still another way is to break up the task into smaller time commitments. In this way, the student doesn't get too bored before being allowed to go to something else, but is nonetheless required to come back in a timely manner to finish.

93. D: The teacher should first instruct the class on the subject matter, then the class should discuss it, and then the students should engage in independent activity. This order insures that the students have the most opportunity to absorb the new material before attempting to complete a related assignment on their own.

94. B: Authentic assessment techniques are designed to build higher-order thinking skills because they require students to construct their own answers instead of choosing from preselected answers. They also allow for the possibility that multiple "correct" answers are possible because students bring different perspectives and prior experiences to the material. They typically measure student performance over an extended period of time and are graded on a criterion-referenced basis (e.g., students are compared to an objective standard, rather than being directly compared to one another).

95. C: Do not interrupt the flow of your class when only a couple of students need more time. However, do make sure the two slower students do not get lost in the shuffle. Set aside a few minutes after class, or while the other students are doing seatwork, to catch them up. Answer A could needlessly traumatize the two slower students. Answer B would not be fair to the other students, and would interfere with the flow of your lesson plan. However, if a majority of your students are having trouble, then it might be worth spending more time on the subject. Answer D would discourage the two students from learning unless the activity is a timed test.

96. D: Different students respond to different kinds of stimuli. A classroom environment that stimulates the mind in several different ways is more likely to help more students to learn effectively.

97. C: The teacher should try rephrasing the question before telling students the answer. Often, students fail to answer because they simply don't understand what information the teacher is looking for, rather than because they actually don't know the information. The teacher might try asking the question from a different angle, providing a hint, or using different terminology.

98. C: Constructivism is a learning theory based on the idea that people are actively involved in the learning process, rather than being passive receivers of knowledge. Constructivism suggests that children learn best by solving real-world problems, gathering information, testing ideas, and other active processes, with teachers guiding and scaffolding them along the way.

99. B: Putting up a general outline will make it easier for the students to follow your talk. Answer A would likely make it harder for the students to follow your lesson. Answer C would also be disruptive. An occasional question to a student who is not paying attention is fine, but doing this too much will cause your lesson to veer off schedule, and may also interfere with other students' note taking. Answer D could also lead to confusion. After all, your goal is for all of your students to have the same level of understanding by the end of the lesson.

100. B: Learning to constructively sort out differences is an important life skill that is worth pursuing in class. Answer A denies the students a chance to benefit from a true discussion. Answer C sends the wrong message. Instead, you should let students know that they will be graded on their level of class participation. Answer D would have the same stifling effect as answer A.

101. D: The teachers' best option for improving students' overall performance on the test, including students who are not struggling with math, would be to find creative ways to incorporate math instruction into other subject areas, and to offer optional math tutoring during lunch and after school. This approach includes all students, so that students who are meeting the standard also have the opportunity to improve their performance. In addition, it does not detract from students' learning in other critical subject areas, or deprive students who are performing satisfactorily of math instruction.

102. A: Singing a song is the answer because this is a pleasant activity that the children enjoy and that helps them to relax. Singing a song is good for a break, especially a break that transitions into a new lesson or activity. Although some songs may also enhance a lesson, the students perceive singing a fun song as just that: fun. Packing up to go home is a routine activity that is part of the classroom management structure. Playing math games is an activity that is directly related to the math curriculum and reinforces a lesson. Taking a field trip is also related to the curriculum and is supposed to be designed to illustrate or enhance a lesson.

103. A: A primary goal of acceptable use policies regarding school computers is to deter students and school employees from accessing inappropriate information or engaging in illegal activities using school computers. Such policies are not educational, and do not teach students about copyright law or plagiarism (C). They cannot prevent computer users from accidentally stumbling upon inappropriate material while using the Internet (B). Transferring documents created on school computers to home computers (D) is not generally a violation of acceptable use policies, since it typically involves creating a document for a school assignment, saving it on a disc or flash drive, and saving it on the student's home computer.

104. C: Asking questions directly to the quieter student will force them to participate. It will also encourage them to participate more on their own if they do not want to be called on directly. Answer A will have little effect, other than to stifle students who are participating, as they should. Answer B will create a tense and distasteful atmosphere that will not foster very productive class discussion. Answer D will only serve to encourage the more active students to participate even more than before.

105. A: Silence can mean a number of things in different cultures. In the dominant American culture, silence often indicates embarrassment and regret, but in many other cultures it may symbolize power, respect, reference, and self-control. Before ascribing a particular value and reason behind the silence to a student, it is essential to determine if the student views silence in this manner. The student may actually not know the answer or be unsure of how to communicate. Being careful not to generalize is important to ensuring students are not stereotyped.

106. C: Preparing to argue both sides of the debate develops higher-order thinking skills by promoting students' awareness of competing viewpoints. While organizational skills (D), self-confidence (B), and autonomy all grow during the middle school years, this exercise is most useful for fostering students' growing awareness of multiple viewpoints.

107. A: Of the four options, asking the students to write down the instructions would be least effective. Having students write down the directions as she explains them does not provide Ms. Fry with any way of knowing whether the students have comprehended the directions or have recorded them correctly. Also, writing is challenging for some students and can distract them from the content of what is being explained.

108. D: In the case of *Plyler v. Doe* (1982), the U.S. Supreme Court ruled that undocumented immigrant children have the same right to a free public education as U.S. citizens and permanent residents. The Court also ruled that schools are prohibited from asking students and/or their parents about the students' immigration status (A); from requiring proof that students are in the U.S. legally, or attempting to document student status (B); and from denying students access based on undocumented status (C).

109. B: Knowing it is considered bad manners to steal porridge best reflects knowledge of cultural conventions. Knowing narrative structure (A) would be reflected by understanding how a story is organized and its component parts. Knowing grammar and vocabulary (C) would be reflected by understanding how sentences are constructed to convey particular meanings, as opposed to other meanings or no meaning; and what meanings various vocabulary words are used to express. Knowing general information (D) would be reflected by, for example, knowing that a house built from bricks will be stronger than a house built from straw.

110. D: Rate, accuracy, and prosody. Fluent readers are able to read smoothly and comfortably at a steady pace (rate). The more quickly a child reads, the greater the chance of leaving out a word or substituting one word for another (for example, *sink* instead of *shrink*). Fluent readers are able to maintain accuracy without sacrificing rate. Fluent readers also stress important words in a text, group words into rhythmic phrases, and read with intonation (prosody).

111. D: Setting an objective without a specific time or amount limit would leave students wondering if there will ever be an end to the task. A common error when writing a criterion is to set it too low, so answer A would be the correct way to write a criterion: setting performance standards high enough to meet skills expectations, especially in reading, writing, and math. Another common error is to set the criterion arbitrarily; for example, setting the accuracy rate for 80% every time, no matter the difficulty of the task, or asking that a task be performed in too short a time. Answer B is correct in directing that the teacher set realistic standards and time limits. Answer C is also a correct way to set the criterion at the right level, gradually increasing expectations for accuracy in a skill; for example, 50% by October, 65% by November, and so on.

112. A: Allowing students to discuss the questions in pairs gives students the opportunity to try out their answers in a "safe" environment before stating them in front of the class. This will make students more comfortable participating in the discussion, thus making it more effective.

113. B: If the 5th graders are doing less demanding work than the 3rd graders, then communication has broken down among the teachers or between the principal and teachers about the level of work that is expected of all students at that school. Students and parents alike will be wondering why the 5th graders are not being expected to do more than 3rd graders as evidence of their skills and knowledge progress. Answer A indicates effective communication if the students know the lesson's objective; such knowledge is required for good teaching. Answer C indicates that the 5th grade teachers have communicated effectively with each other and are working as a team for organized instruction. Answer D describes a situation that is good practice for communicating to students the expectations and standards of an assignment.

114. A: It greatly helps the learning process when the teacher illustrates how the new material fits together with what the class has already learned. This also serves to remind students of past lessons and to keep the information fresh. Answer B can be useful occasionally, but is not practical as a daily option. Answer C would substantially raise tension in the classroom, and would do little to assist the students in processing information. Answer D is certainly helpful, but once more it does not substitute for a teacher tying things together at the end of a lesson.

115. C: By giving students detailed feedback on their performance and providing opportunities to incorporate the feedback and demonstrate improvement, a teacher can give students a sense of control over their learning. For example, a teacher might provide students with detailed feedback on an essay, and then give them a chance to rewrite and improve it to achieve a higher grade.

116. A: Planning out the lesson yourself in writing is the only way to ensure that all of the parts of your lesson will fit together logically. The more time you put into your preparations, the better your lesson will go in the classroom. Answer B is unreliable for this purpose. The students do not know what your goals are for the lesson. Occasionally checking in with your students is useful, but not as a substitute for lesson planning. Answer C is equally ineffective, and will bore even your best students to tears. Most classes need to go beyond the scope of the textbook, and many classes use more than one book. Answer D is a very poor way to teach. Each teacher needs to customize his own lesson. This will make it more interesting, and will take into account aspects of your school's particular curriculum, as well as the needs of your specific students.

117. B: Mr. Rogers' practices are most relevant to promoting understanding and empathy among students from diverse cultures and preventing student conflicts by helping them express their diverse viewpoints, relate to each other's perspectives, and discuss their emotions in the school context. The question does not identify any students as experiencing cultural identity crises (A). While it does describe Mr. Rogers as teaching English language use and academic subject content, it does not describe any practices for specifically improving academic achievements (C). It does not describe any practices for specifically acknowledging and addressing student linguistic diversity (D).

118. A: If you are teaching a class while relevant current events are taking place, it is well worth the while to devote a significant amount of time to addressing them in class. There are few things that motivate students as much as seeing how what they are learning applies to "real life," especially in the present. Answer B is a mistake. The teacher should be flexible, make judgments on a case-by-case basis, as to how much time is appropriate to devote. Answer C is a great idea, but should not be a substitute for in class-discussion. The students need to hear the teacher's explanation of events before taking on extracurricular assignments independently. Answer D is once again not very practical, since some events are more relevant than others.

119. B: This information will help the teachers plan their instruction based on the strengths and needs of the incoming students. Standardized test information should not be the sole basis on which students are given remedial instruction (A); their class performance should be strongly considered as well. D is incorrect because team teaching can be effective regardless of how well or poorly students perform on standardized tests, and C is incorrect because the decision to repeat a grade typically does not involve a student's future teachers, and should not be based solely on standardized test results.

120. D: Many parents assume that as their children approach adulthood, the parents should step back and let them make the children make own mistakes. While children at this age do need to have a little more freedom and responsibility, this age range is actually a particularly critical time in students' development and they need the involvement and guidance of their families more than ever. A teacher does have the power to help change this by reaching out to the parents and creating more opportunities for them to be involved in class activities. It also helps to try and get your school more involved with parents in general.

121. A: Environmental print is the print people see in their everyday lives. For children, this may include restaurant logos, food labels, and street signs. Environmental print helps children understand that print has meaning, and reading familiar words can boost reading confidence. The remaining options provide students with opportunities to read other types of meaningful words, but not environmental print.

122. C: Before punishing the students or assuming that they don't understand the material, Mr. Tollison should ensure that all of the students know what the homework assignment is and correctly record it before leaving the classroom. Students may not complete the assignment correctly if they fail to write it down, especially if the assigned problems are shouted out hastily at the end of class.

123. A: Textbooks are often dry and abstract in the way that they present material. Having the students read some first-person accounts of events, or other less formal materials, can bring the subject to life, and may even encourage students to read more on their own. Answer B will be of little use if the material is dry. Answer C is irrelevant, since the question regards helping students to learn rather than how to evaluate their progress. Answer D is a bit overly ambitious to pull off in a classroom; however, it is rooted in a very good idea. Having students act out certain events can be a very effective way to get students more involved emotionally. However, the events chosen should lend themselves to reenactment within the space available, and must be closely supervised to ensure realism.

124. D: This is a classic situation in which a teacher observes a dangerous pattern in a student's performance. The parents should be consulted as soon as possible. Answer A represents a situation that is already out of control. The parents should have been contacted long before, since it will now be very hard for her to save her grade. Answer B represents a situation that should continue to be monitored, but which does not yet rise to the need of contacting a parent. Answer C represents a situation which might be better referred to the assistant principal's office, since the student is probably in violation of the school dress code, and not just of a class rule.

125. C: Rubrics are effective assessment tools because they provide students with more specific feedback. They do this by including evaluations of two or more specific learning objectives or performance categories within a single assignment, as opposed to providing one undifferentiated grade for a complex activity. Rubrics should include at least two categories (for example, content/organization and spelling/grammar for an essay), and there is no limit to the number of categories that a rubric can have. Since even the simplest assignment, such as completing a math problem, is composed of several components (applying the correct formula, calculating the answer correctly, and writing the problem neatly, for example), rubrics can be used for grading many different types of class work.

126. B: Classrooms come in a variety of shapes and sizes. Moreover, the arrangement that works for one class will not necessarily work for another. Answer C, with the desks facing the chalkboard, seems logical and might work in many cases, but you need to consider the needs of your class first. For example, some teachers prefer to use an overhead projector instead of a chalkboard. Also, some classrooms have more than one chalkboard. Answer A is not a good idea unless there really is a major source of distraction outside the window. Answer D is absurd. School administrators do not spend any time optimizing the floor plans of classrooms. The previous teacher's arrangement will not necessarily work for you.

127. B: After removing a student from class for seriously disruptive behavior, no teacher may be obligated to take the student back, and no principal may coerce you to do so. It is your decision alone to make.

128. C: the best approach would be for Mrs. Li to take the learning disabled students to a quiet area and facilitate a 15 minute group reading discussion while the other students write. Since the objective of the writing assignment is actually to assess the students' reading comprehension, not their writing ability, this can be accomplished orally as well as in writing. Although giving students more time to complete the assignment would be appropriate if this were an assignment assessing writing ability, it would be unfair to ask students to complete extra homework due to their learning disability if there is another assessment method readily available.

129. B: By singling out students who may dress differently due to cultural or religious differences, those students may feel ostracized or different from other students. It is important for schools to closely examine their dress code policies along with other school policies to determine if they are inclusive of all cultures and backgrounds. Although it is possible that the student may feel unique, it will most likely not make her feel special. Moreover, because she is the only student in the school who wears head garbs, she will most likely notice the differences. Especially in middle school, students are developmentally aware of their peers and may seek to fit in rather than stand out.

130. C: Though many people would look the other way, Mr. Calhoun would be committing an ethical violation by selling products such as Girl Scout cookies on school property. It may not seem like much of an offense, but it does not benefit the school in any way, and some parents might complain about a teacher who is selling sweets to their children. Moreover, Mr. Calhoun's students might even get the idea that if they do not buy Mr. Calhoun's cookies, that they will not get good grades.

Thank You

We at Mometrix would like to extend our heartfelt thanks to you, our friend and patron, for allowing us to play a part in your journey. It is a privilege to serve people from all walks of life who are unified in their commitment to building the best future they can for themselves.

The preparation you devote to these important testing milestones may be the most valuable educational opportunity you have for making a real difference in your life. We encourage you to put your heart into it—that feeling of succeeding, overcoming, and yes, conquering will be well worth the hours you've invested.

We want to hear your story, your struggles and your successes, and if you see any opportunities for us to improve our materials so we can help others even more effectively in the future, please share that with us as well. **The team at Mometrix would be absolutely thrilled to hear from you!** So please, send us an email (support@mometrix.com) and let's stay in touch.

If you feel as though you need additional help, please check out the other resources we offer:

Study Guide: http://MometrixStudyGuides.com/TExES

Flashcards: http://MometrixFlashcards.com/TExES